T0301544

Entrepreneurial Seoulite

perspectives on
CONTEMPORARY
K O R E A

SERIES EDITORS: NOJIN KWAK AND YOUNGJU RYU

Perspectives on Contemporary Korea is devoted to scholarship that advances the understanding of critical issues in contemporary Korean society, culture, politics, and economy. The series is sponsored by The Nam Center for Korean Studies at the University of Michigan.

Hallyu 2.0: The Korean Wave in the Age of Social Media
   Sangjoon Lee and Abé Mark Nornes, editors

Smartland Korea: Mobile Communication, Culture, and Society
   Dal Yong Jin

Transgression in Korea: Beyond Resistance and Control
   Juhn Y. Ahn, editor

Cultures of Yusin: South Korea in the 1970s
   Youngju Ryu, editor

Entrepreneurial Seoulite: Culture and Subjectivity in Hongdae, Seoul
   Mihye Cho

Entrepreneurial Seoulite

Culture and Subjectivity in Hongdae, Seoul

Mihye Cho

UNIVERSITY OF MICHIGAN PRESS

Ann Arbor

Published in the United States of America by
the University of Michigan Press
Printed and bound by CPI Group (UK) Ltd, Croydon, CR0 4YY

First published February 2019

A CIP catalog record for this book is available from the British Library.

ISBN 978-0-472-07416-7 (hardcover : alk. paper)
ISBN 978-0-472-05416-9 (paper : alk. paper)
ISBN 978-0-472-12558-6 (ebook)

This work was supported by the Academy of Korean Studies (KSPS) Grant funded by the Korean
Government (MOE) (AKS-2011-BAA-2102).

Contents

Preface

The Asian financial crisis hit South Korea in 1997 just as I was about to graduate from the university. I gave up the idea of finding a regular job while my friend who was studying English literature took over her father's bankrupt company. My friend was liquidating the company all by herself because her father became a credit defaulter and was thus unable to access any bank account. She also started selling her used clothes on eBay, an online marketplace, to support her family. She soon began to purchase new clothes from wholesalers and sell them through a variety of online markets.

Another friend took a leave of absence from college and left for Japan to help her mother. Her father's business went bankrupt, too, and her mother found work in Osaka with their relative who was running an amusement arcade, or pachinko parlor. My friend sat at the pachinko counter, exchanging coins for customers.

One of my high school classmates who was majoring in fashion design began to work as an assistant at a wedding gown boutique in Gangnam, Seoul. The classmate had fainted twice due to the heavy workload. She soon quit the job and left for a small garment company at Dongdaemun Market, a well-known fashion mall for both retailers and designers located in the middle of Seoul. There, she designed clothes for wholesalers. She started her own business within a few years, running between factories in China and wholesalers in Japan. All these events began when we were twenty-two years old.

Only two years earlier, at the age of twenty, my friends and I went to Hongdae in Seoul to meet other friends, head to clubs and gigs, attend study groups, and roam the streets. Hongdae was our territory, the place for Generation Xers. We talked about alternative music, films, backpacking, study abroad, Pierre Bourdieu, simulacra, and feminism. Within a short span of time, however, we found ourselves as contingent laborers.

Now we discussed bankruptcy, provisional attachment, bad credit, and illegal migration. We still went to Hongdae to take a breather. When the Asian financial crisis, what Koreans popularly refer to as the International Monetary Fund (IMF) period, hit, we did not know what it was about exactly. As with everyone else, my friends and I exerted ourselves just to get by.

Two decades have passed since the IMF period. I currently work in Singapore. My friend who was liquidating her father's company has completely cleared all business liabilities and is now a full-time housewife with two children. My friend who was working at the pachinko parlor in Osaka is now an assistant professor in New York. My designer friend is currently running an online takeout lunch box shop based in Seoul. We are all getting on fine with our lives. Or so it seems.

My friends and I might be the lucky ones to have survived the moment of creative destruction in the aftermath of the financial crisis. But I harbor mixed feelings. I have learned to be entrepreneurial in order to survive. In so doing, however, I have overlooked the precarious lives of others. Becoming an entrepreneur, I think, makes life exhausting to the extent that one becomes an uncaring person—one who is incapable of caring for something other than survival.

For quite some time, I used to tell others that I research about Seoul's transformation from a Fordist to a post-Fordist city. In fact, this urban phenomenon entails the transformation of personhood, from a Fordist person to a post-Fordist person. I had not imagined myself living in the United Kingdom, Germany, or Singapore, chasing after scholarships, research grants, and jobs. I was surprised when my friend ventured into online retailing. I looked in awe at my designer friend's bravery when she interacted with male laborers in China. I respected my friend who had to work in the pachinko parlor but then won a scholarship to study in New York and remitted part of her stipend to her family in Korea. Indeed, we have been fully occupied with a new socialization process, learning to be entrepreneurial and thereby becoming post-financial-crisis or post-Fordist people.

Musing on the phenomenon called "Hongdae culture" for almost fifteen years, I have come face to face with the legacies of the democratic movements in the 1980s, the hybridism of leftism and neoliberalism during the 1990s and the 2000s, and the triumph of neoliberalism in the 2010s. I realize now that I have been contemplating the transformation of Korea from the vantage point of anxious middle-class Koreans.

A sense of indebtedness as well as desperation have underlain my research. Such indebtedness originated from my uneasiness that my research site was neither the factories of labor disputes nor the streets of civil activism. The desperation was based on my fear of ending up as one of the numerous educated, unemployed youth. The desire to express that my schizophrenic middle-class sensibility—that is, the coexistence of an instinct for survival and a self-reflexivity that has kept me alert and striving to become a good citizen—has driven this research on Hongdae. Studying Hongdae has been therapeutic for me in recovering from the shock of the financial crisis.

I am neither radical nor idealistic. I do not even dream of discarding the current capitalism and devising an alternative. Yet I am concerned about whether younger people will also have to endure this exhausting socialization process. The mixed feelings of shame and responsibility have driven me to write about Hongdae, the place continually becoming something new.

Acknowledgments

Many people have shared their stories about Hongdae with me. While not all of them are included in this book, these storytellers were all kind and empathetic to entrust their tales with a novice researcher. I thank them for their hospitality and sincerity. Special thanks go to Cho Y., Choi J., Ra D., Lee M., Kim Y., and Ryu J., who have helped me significantly since I commenced my fieldwork for this research. In a later stage of my research, Sung G., Jung M., and Cha W. inspired me with their frankness and insights.

I thank my Ph.D. supervisor, Joanna Pfaff-Czarnecka. She acknowledged my thirst to write about actor-oriented social events and helped me embark on the first step of my research. I thank the support from the International Graduate School in Sociology (IGSS) at Bielefeld University. With the IGSS's scholarship and travel funds, I was able to conduct the early stage of the research.

Tracey Skelton, as a senior in the area of geography, has guided me on how to engage in issues of place. I had invaluable dialogues about "ethnography in the meantime" with anthropologist Michael Fischer. Thanks go to Susan Silbey, who has inspired me with her pride in being a sociologist. Because of her, I accomplished a fresh reading of Weber. These scholars have helped me establish my scholarly identity as an urban sociologist. Since then, my research about Hongdae has entered a new stage.

I am grateful for all the support from the Singapore University of Technology and Design (SUTD), where I have worked in recent years. With research funds from SUTD, I was able to conduct the later stage of research for this book. The senior engineers at SUTD have thrown me into the world of interdisciplinary research and thanks to them, I have co-researched city and society with engineers and architects. They have given me opportunities to experience the intersection of structures in my everyday life. All the students in my course on social science theories have stimulated me to find fresh meanings in old theories.

At the University of Michigan Press, Christopher Dreyer and Nojin Kwak kept the book on track. I am truly grateful for their confidence in my research and all their support in the completion of this book.

My research was made possible thanks to Chona Lazo and Riza Castillo. They have provided wonderful child care, which enabled me to pursue my research and writing. Ong Yanchun carefully read many versions of the manuscript and helped me improve my writing. I appreciate Mun Suhyun's camaraderie. She has given me invaluable comments on my arguments. Tomoo and Yui Kikuchi have been endless suppliers of encouragement and support. Last, I thank Koreans of past generations who fought for justice and freedom so that I was able to be part of Generation X and write this book.

Introduction

This book might be read as a memoir on Hongdae, a place located in Seoul, based on my observations as a member of South Korea's Generation X. I am an ethnographer who subsequently became an entrepreneur. I define entrepreneurialism not as business knowledge and skills but as a disposition in which one regards the self as a risk-taking agency imposing self-organization and self-responsibility not only on economic undertakings but also on the lifestyle at large. During the 1990s, Hongdae became widely known as a cool place associated with discourses on Hongdae culture—including alternative music, independent labels, and club culture. Today, Hongdae is well known for its youth culture and nightlife, as well as its gentrification.[1] Although I approach Hongdae culture seriously, this book is about neither subculture nor gentrification in Seoul. Rather, its focus is on the relationship between the "ideology that justifies engagement in capitalism"[2] and "subjectification processes."[3] This book aims to understand the project to institutionalize a cultural district in Hongdae as a demonstration of the coevolution of ideologies (or "a set of shared beliefs inscribed in institutions")[4] and citizenship in a society undergoing rapid liberalization—politically, culturally, and economically.

A cultural turn began in Korea during the 1990s amid the economic prosperity brought on by state-led industrialization in the previous decades and the democratization and liberalization after the collapse of the military dictatorship in 1987. Cultural critiques, which emerged as an alternative to social movements, proliferated to advocate freedom and autonomy of individuals against regulatory systems and institutions attached to the previous regimes.

This cultural turn spread to the spheres of economic policy and urban governance after the 1997 Asian financial crisis as Korea embarked on massive economic restructuring including the liberalization of financial, labor, and real estate markets as part of crisis management. Meanwhile, the creative and information technology industries were heavily promoted as the new engines of economic growth that would spearhead a knowledge-oriented economy.[5] The IMF bailout, widely regarded by Koreans as the coercion of international institutions, infused the financial crisis with a sense of national identity crisis. Culture thus became regarded as the emblem of national autonomy in an environment in which the economy was perceived as exogenous and uncontrollable. Creativity, often reified as culture and the culture industry, inspired city governments to modify manufacturing-oriented, compartmentalized urban planning to drive new engines of urban development. Seoul has sought to transform itself from a megacity into a world-class global city equipped with vitality, infrastructures, and cutting-edge knowledge industries. In short, culture/creativity became a focal point for advancing liberalized civil society, economic restructuring, and politics against globalization.

What kinds of logics guide individuals in their engagement with new urban realities? Juxtaposing the cultural turn as the dissemination of a new spirit of post-financial-crisis Korea, this book interrogates the challenges to achieve symbiosis between culture and economy and the struggles to seek new citizen subjectivities amid new urbanism brought by the transformations after the financial crisis. I begin by examining the old realities as well as the new ones that emerged.

Hongdae and the Spirit of the 1990s

Toward the end of 1993, an advertisement for a cosmetic product called Twin X was aired on TV. It contained no sound. Instead, the following phrases were projected on a black-and-white background image of two young men: "Who am I?"; "Limitless Directing"; "Reason < Feeling"; and "I, Generation X." Who makes up Generation X? The emergence of "indeterminable" young people received attention as a social issue on a TV news program in 1994.[6] The reporter defined this group as the Generation X, which came to refer to those who were born in the 1970s and reached their twenties in the 1990s. They were said to be fortunate enough to enjoy prosperity and freedom, a gift from the warlike democratization movements throughout the 1980s fought by an earlier generation. Indeed, the Twin X advertisement appeared when the first civilian government (Kim Young Sam's government from 1993 to 1998) came to power.

Since then, Generation X has become synonymous with the Korea of the 1990s.

Korean society in the 1990s differed vastly from that of the 1980s. A novelist who experienced her twenties in the 1980s and her thirties in the 1990s remarks that it is impossible to explain Korean society in the 1990s with the language of the 1980s or to understand Korean society in the 1980s with the sentiment of the 1990s. Indeed, when she was a university student, "AIDS" meant "Anti Imperial Direct Struggle" among the students; she assumes that nobody in the 1990s would have understood it in the same way.[7] Meanwhile, Hongdae culture was often singled out as an example of a new cultural phenomenon in the 1990s. Cho, a guitar player, magazine editor, manager of a cultural event company, and part-time waiter, commented to me that those "wandering intellectuals" looking for a new subject in social sciences as Marxism went out of fashion had flocked to Hongdae.[8]

As if dutifully representing Generation X, I bought a bottle of Twin X in 1994—the year I entered the university. I commuted from home to the campus in Seoul via the metropolitan subways, where I had to pass two satellite cities to reach my destination. I look back on this commuting experience as the starting point for my urban ethnography. I became a participant observer of Seoul, crossing the border between non-Seoul and Seoul. As soon as I stepped onto the university grounds, I sensed the spatial division of my cohort. My peers were divided into three groups: those who lived in Gangnam, or southern Seoul below the Han River; those from Gangbuk, or northern Seoul above the river; and the rest who came from the non-Seoul world. I was one of a few students from the metropolitan area between Seoul and non-Seoul. Students from Gangnam generally lived in the affluent apartment complexes. They graduated from the same schools, wore upmarket branded clothes that were hard to find outside Seoul, and commuted on the same buses. They looked exclusive. Although Psy made "Gangnam Style" world famous in a song in 2012, I encountered Gangnam and its urbanism in the 1990s.

I also witnessed the last moments of student activism. A handful of senior students introduced themselves to me as "NL" (for National Liberation) and "PD" (for People's Democracy). I was told that the NL worked for national unification and the PD for laborers. The seniors taught me protest songs, such as "March for the Beloved" ("Imŭl wihan haengjin'gok") "From Seoul to Pyongyang," "From the Wilderness" ("Kwangyaesŏ"), and "La International." They made me read Marxist books and brought me to a half-demolished squatters' shantytown. They participated in street demonstrations against the Uruguay Round[9] and the opening of the agricultural product market to free trade.

I doubted these seniors from the NL and the PD knew what they were doing. Their slogans about national emancipation and labor revolution sounded pretentious and anachronistic. The majority of my peers did not join in student activism. In fact, university students stopped marching on the streets. Rather, they organized study groups to prepare for bar exams, civil service exams, and the TOEFL (Test of English as a Foreign Language). Globalization, or *sekyewha* in Korean, was the mantra of the time, and English was treated as the second official language. University students joined social clubs for backpacking and learning English. I was also skeptical toward these interest groups and regarded their members as conformists. I felt that I belonged to neither the pretentious activists nor the vulgar conformists.

Consequently, I began to hang out in Hongdae, which was known for its free, experimental, and creative atmosphere. I went to a live club called Drug when it first opened its doors. Live clubs were the places to hear music performed live, and they produced the genre that came to be called Hongdae music. Drug is known as the birthplace of the alternative, independent music scene. A cultural critic described Hongdae as a place where the avant-garde and the kitsch mixed.[10] I often went to Hongdae because I neither fitted in with nor liked Gangnam style. Yet I felt a sense of ambivalence toward Hongdae. I was able to find what I liked, such as a relaxed and individualistic atmosphere, nonmainstream music, and handmade goods. They were all, in fact, nothing but products with Hongdae flair—namely, "Hongdae style."

The same year I entered the university, the Seongsu Bridge connecting Gangnam and Gangbuk collapsed. The incident was regarded as an unprecedented manmade disaster. The bridge had been built in 1979 when Gangnam, then a rural area, was undergoing rapid development into a massive new town driven by conglomerates. In the 1970s, to attract middle-class families to settle in Gangnam, large-scale infrastructure projects such as the construction of roads and schools were hastily implemented. In the summer of 1995, Sampoong Department Store, located in the heart of Gangnam, collapsed because of illegal modification of building design and materials. The accident caused almost fifteen hundred casualties. Together, these manmade accidents signaled the breakdown of Seoul's developmental urbanism.

Since the Korean War (1950–1953), the authoritarian regimes had focused on the provision of housing and building of industrial infrastructures. Seoul thus became a "spatial machine" designed to embrace a surge of rural migrants, and developers built high-rise apartment blocks to accommodate them.[11] The government had distributed public resources unevenly. This is especially evident in the area of housing, where speculative developers, usually conglomerates, directed urban development with the institutional support of the state. While the central government determined the strategic allocation of public resources, it had overlooked the equitable distribution and provision of social welfare. In short, developmental and military regimes maximized economic development by creating new towns, free economic zones, and mobility infrastructures.[12] Even though the democratization movements had replaced the military state with the civilian state, urban policy—which facilitated the capital accumulation of construction companies and wealth creation of affluent classes—continued well into the 1990s with meager reform.

In 1997 the Asian financial crisis hit Korea. This crisis is popularly referred to as the IMF crisis because of the implementation of the IMF's adjustment programs for crisis management.[13] The adjustment programs focused on trade liberalization and deregulation of the financial and labor markets[14] and was seen as an infringement on Korean national autonomy by international institutions. The economic prosperity driven by the developmental state in the past decades was shattered. Massive economic restructuring, which entailed layoffs and prevalence of contingent employment, proceeded in the aftermath. Homelessness, breakdown of the family, unemployment, and suicide emerged as pressing social problems. Signboards for going-out-of-business sales appeared everywhere. Personally, at that time I had given up on the idea of finding a regular job. I started working instead as a tuition teacher, or private tutor, to give myself time to think about what I should do. Within just four years, we Generation Xers had witnessed the Korean version of "all that is solid melts into air."[15]

While working as a flexible laborer, I visited Hongdae more often than ever. To my surprise, given the economic situation, Hongdae was filled with young people, especially in the dance clubs. These clubs were typically small, and the dance music was played by DJs. For about five dollars, people could purchase an entrance ticket that allowed them to linger without ordering drinks. Dance clubs were registered as restaurants because of venue size and tax issues, and strictly speaking, they were illegal: they violated public hygienic legislation because dancing was prohibited in restaurants. On one occasion, I had to evacuate a dance club to evade a police crackdown. Among these clubs, I recall, Sangsoodo was the most exciting as it was hidden within a residential area. There, I met a queer community, cross-dressers, filmmakers, and artists—in other words, the so-called creative class.

University students, young professionals, artists, cultural workers, foreigners, and students who had to return prematurely from their overseas studies because of the financial crisis gathered in Hongdae.[16] The massive reconstruction projects had partially contributed to the congregation of people in Hongdae.[17] After the collapse of the Seongsu Bridge, the rebuilding of the Dangsan Railway Bridge across the Han River began in 1997 because of increased safety concerns. Such large-scale infrastructure projects lasted for several years and resulted in reduced mobility within inner-city areas in the meantime. Young people, who depended relatively heavily on public transportation for mobility, were particularly affected. Thus, they gathered in Hongdae rather than traveled to Gangnam.

In 1999 I flew to the United Kingdom to pursue a postgraduate course. There, I was directly exposed to Cool Britannia, the global success of the British culture industry. In fact, my direct exposure to British subcultures started when I spent one year in Sheffield as an exchange student between 1996 and 1997, on the eve of the Asian financial crisis. Sheffield, together with neighboring Manchester, was the base of Britpop indie bands. The city, once a steel industry town, was being reinvigorated as a postindustrial city with mega shopping malls, new street trams, loft apartments, and cultural quarters. I observed a Western version of postindustrial urban restructuring. Although it was coincidental that I successively roamed Hongdae and then inner-city Sheffield, two hip places across Asia and Europe, it was my first experience of comparative global urbanism.

During my postgraduate study, I was surprised to meet senior students from Korea: an official and a researcher sent by the Ministry of Culture and Tourism, whose studies were sponsored by the Kim Dae Jung government (1998–2003). We talked about British indie bands and the culture industry, and I was pleasantly surprised because I had assumed Korea's cultural institutions were mainly concerned with traditional culture and conservation. Subsequently, I realized that this encounter might have offered a direct observation on policy transfer or communication between those policies that promoted Cool Britannia and those that fostered the Korean wave (K-wave) and K-pop.[18]

After completing my studies, I began to work as a label manager at a multinational music corporation based in Seoul. This time I visited Hongdae to conduct market surveys. Clubbing in Hongdae became a fashionable leisure activity among young people. The popularity of Hongdae clubs increased significantly with the incredible success of Club Day. In

2001 four clubs started selling a single ticket for entry to all four clubs under the slogan "Clubber's Harmony."[19] Other clubs subsequently joined the event, and the fourth Friday of each month became designated as Club Day. The turnout was tremendous.

Working as a label manager allowed me to observe the onset of the digitization of music and the exploitation of a so-called creative underclass.[20] Most of the musicians, club managers, art directors, performers, designers, curators, and artists whom I met held university degrees. Some of them had master's and doctoral degrees. Yet they were poorly paid. They neither earned regular incomes nor received state welfare.

I began to think that the music industry had no future since people would stop buying physical music albums soon. Unless I became a copyright owner, I would end up as part of the meretricious creative underclass. Although I do not discuss the issue of the creative underclass in depth in this book, Hongdae could have been one of the places where an immobile creative underclass came to live, work, and play in the aftermath of the financial crisis.

In 2002 I finally marched on the streets: the 2002 FIFA World Cup brought Koreans out to occupy the streets once more. The World Cup was regarded as an opportunity to rebuild Korea's staggering economy and restore national pride after being a recipient of the IMF's aid. The city government promoted Hongdae to its international visitors as the leading edge of Seoul's culture. Indeed, Hongdae was well placed to become the number one cultural destination as it was located near the World Cup stadium and had full urban amenities. As a result, Hongdae clubs and Club Day observed an "explosive growth."[21]

I embarked on my doctoral research just as the World Cup ended. My initial research project focused on the debates on Korea's transition from modernity to postmodernity, with Hongdae as my empirical research site. As is the usual experience of most doctoral students, I realized that my initial research topic should be discarded. The real issue was not the transition from modernism to postmodernism; rather, it was about new subjectification processes[22] and the transition from Generation X to something different.

Hongdae and a New Spirit of Capitalism

Hongdae, a subcultural area, became an object of municipal administration in 2000 when the city government commissioned its umbrella institute, the Seoul Development Institute (SDI), to explore Seoul's promotion for the World Cup.[23] The city government harnessed the slogan "culture World Cup, civic World Cup, and environmental World Cup" to promote Seoul. The task force organized by the SDI produced a report titled *Place Marketing of the [2002] World Cup Strategic Areas: Schemes for Vitalizing Culture in Hongdae*. Organized as a form of public-private partnership, the task force comprised a number of researchers from the SDI, a civic activist previously engaged in labor and environmental activism, and a cultural program planner based in Hongdae who pioneered the local techno club scene.

The report noted that new buildings, the influx of franchise businesses and amenities, and increasing rental rates were pushing small-scale subcultural facilities and businesses out of Hongdae. After the 1997 financial crisis, the government, with a budget in deficit, introduced liquidity support measures, tax reduction, and deregulation of real estate transactions to revitalize the real estate markets. It was noted that the price of real estate plunged 30 percent on average after the financial crisis.[24] Soon, however, the combination of the deregulation of land usage and financial markets resulted in the influx of speculative capital into the real estate markets.[25] This led to real estate bubbles and inflation: between 2000 and 2002, the prices of housing increased some 20 to 30 percent on average in Seoul and the metropolitan area.[26] Although the term "gentrification" was not widely used at that time, the report in fact documented incipient gentrification.

Under such circumstances, the World Cup was regarded as an occasion to upgrade a cultural infrastructure and harness institutional support to promote local cultural scenes.[27] The SDI report proposed the creation of a cultural precinct in Hongdae in order to incentivize subcultural facilities and business establishments. This proposal had in mind a cultural policy called the cultural district (CD). The CD policy was introduced in 2000 to complement the existing cultural policy, which focused on conservation.[28] The CD policy was conceived as part of the wider efforts to forge a cultural city where cultural sites, cultural life, and the culture industry are interconnected organically.[29]

Seen in this light, the making of a cultural precinct shares the generic idea advocated by promotors of the creative city thesis:[30] the success of a city depends on human creativity, and therefore a city should endorse the enabling environments where human creativity is transmitted to urban milieus and industrial innovations. The association between human creativity and a city's success is closely related to the shift of capital accumulation processes from mass production to differentiated productions in conjunction with network, financial, and technological development in the 1990s.[31] In other words, profit-generation has occurred in the knowledge-intensified industries, which mainly create added value from certain qualities of human beings. Therefore, the capacity of laborers to synthesize personal traits and skills to create products is emphasized. Accordingly, a new meritocratic approach to value autonomy, creativity, and flexibility has emerged as the characteristics of a desirable workforce.[32] Proponents of the creative city thesis basically seek to vitalize urban life by reindustrializing deindustrialized cities, especially with the promotion of knowledge-oriented industries.[33] In so doing, the creative city thesis invokes human creativity to highlight the characteristics of desirable workforces in post-Fordist cities.

The Hongdae report, like the creative city thesis, invokes creativity/culture to make sense of post-Fordist urban transformation. However, this transformation is conditioned by the enmeshment of the financial crisis with the existing social, cultural, and political movements. The Hongdae report explains that the making of the cultural precinct would protect budding subcultural activities and businesses from "competition-driven capitalistic logics," and such protection is seen as the practice of "cultural politics."[34] Interestingly, the report adopts place marketing as "a new strategy that applies marketing skills of business administration to urban regeneration."[35] It suggests that residents, district officials, cultural workers, and businesspeople serve as leading local actors who ought to imagine themselves as "place-marketing agents." Notably, "cultural subjects" are encouraged to imagine themselves as "place imagineers" and "cultural engineers" who can create their own place and culture.[36] In short, becoming place-marketing agents is introduced to counteract and transcend capitalist logics.

It is intriguing that the task force, comprising seemingly liberal and left-leaning participants, recommended marketing as the overarching framework to address the critiques of capitalism and cultural politics. I interpret this incongruous equating of marketing with a corrective force against capitalism as "culture jamming,"[37] a tactic to disrupt mainstream culture and cultural institutions experimented with at the policy level. By advancing subculture as an object of official cultural administration, the Hongdae report was in effect challenging the existing institutional definition of culture confined to established forms of arts, or culture proper. Instead, it imagined subcultural agencies as active citizens who lead their cultural and economic lives autonomously. It also carried a political intention—one that urged subcultural actors to gain legitimate access to institutional resources.

How can creativity, constituted as Hongdae culture, be transmitted to the local economy, and vice versa? In a nutshell, place-marketing Hongdae imagined the symbiosis of culture and economy. However, its solution was discursive and amalgamated mutually incompatible notions. The Hongdae report pitches cultural politics against capitalist logics within the framework of business management. It thus equates cultural politics with the transcendence of market rules via mastering entrepreneurial excellence. The report envisions citizens becoming "marketing agents," "place imagineers," and "cultural engineers"—in short, self-organizing urban entrepreneurs who strive to secure tenancy in a market-cum-city. Imbued with the task of forging symbiosis, the report thus problematizes the self rather than tackles the duality of value—specifically, cultural value vis-à-vis economic value, value as priceless vis-à-vis value as price.[38] The incorporation of critiques of capitalism within a business management framework resulted in the problematization of the self; this happened in Hongdae and in post-financial-crisis Korea more broadly. I argue that the aspirations embedded in place-marketing Hongdae unveil the new urban realities at particular historical junctures in Korea—specifically the transformations wrought by sociocultural and economic liberalization under the banner of the symbiosis between culture and economy.

In the aftermath of Korea's democratization movements, the main concerns of social movements turned from antidictatorship and anti-authoritarianism to individual autonomy and inclusive civic activism. Nongovernmental organizations (NGOs) and civic activists asserted the liberation of individuals from state interference. Kim Dae Jung, leader of democratization activism, became the nation's president in 1998 and sought governance regimes by partnering with the civic sectors.[39] Kim's administration tried to garner civic mediation to implement policies to overcome the financial crisis by increasing the funding to NGOs and civic groups and thus secure their participation in managing governance.[40]

The government followed the IMF's structural adjustment programs, which focused primarily on economic liberalization—notably deregulation and opening Korea to foreign trade.[41] Previously, the military regimes utilized economic crises as opportunities to impose strong governmental intervention. However, the 1997 financial crisis was understood as the outcome of excessive state intervention in markets.[42] Kim's government was thus pressured to transform the state-planned economy into a more liberalized one. Governmental technocrats adopted the requirements of the IMF as a pragmatic process to spur economic restructuring and to boost foreign export.[43] The civic sectors, including former left-leaning activists, advanced the vision of less state intervention and more individual freedom and thus regarded economic restructuring as inevitable. At stake, however, was the implementation of deregulation without preparing for appropriate supervisory measures. This led to the rapid transition of Korea from a nonwelfare state to a neoliberal state in the absence of classical welfare regimes.[44]

Furthermore, the financial crisis drove culture to the fore as representative of Korea's national pride and economic vision.[45] During the 1990s, cultural policy underwent a major shift in its focus from regulation to autonomy, centralization to regionalization, creatorship to consumers, and nationalism to globalization.[46] The promotion of public culture was perceived to negate the effects of the totalitarian and dictatorial regimes on civic life. Concurrently, culture came to represent national autonomy because of an elevated sense of threat posed by international pressure on Korea to embrace free trade on cultural products.[47] This foreboding was heightened by the financial crisis and the IMF regime. All of these developments resulted in a self-contradicting cultural policy that justified (national) cultural exceptionalism from (global) market rules, alongside the commodification of (national) culture for (global) market successes.

This cultural turn was accelerated by the unexpected popularity of Korean dramas in Asia. This phenomenon, widely known as the K-wave, was closely intertwined with the financial crisis. Broadcasting companies' main source of income, advertising sales, dropped significantly as a result of client companies' austerity management. With the exception of Japan, broadcasting companies across Asia suffered from budget-cutting measures as well as currency depreciation. Companies thus began to pay attention to the relatively cheaper media products from Korea, which in turn led to the popularity of Korean cultural products.[48] This K-wave success enhanced the status of culture as a pillar of Korea's national economy.

I juxtapose this cultural turn and the new spirit of post-financial-crisis Korea to elucidate how Hongdae culture became an arena where this new spirit was disseminated and accompanied by the subjectification processes. The new spirit has evolved amid the multifaceted projects of becoming autonomous and liberalistic citizens, subverting elitist cultural institutions, and protecting national economy threatened by "rational others"—specifically the IMF.[49] I argue that creativity, reified as culture, was invoked to connect two different matters—namely, the liberalization of individual autonomy and the liberalization of the workings of capitalism. As a result, creativity/culture has been harnessed to guide how one should engage with the new realities in culturally and economically liberalized Seoul.

Max Weber defines the spirit of capitalism as a set of beliefs and justifications for the capitalist order, expressed in the moral reasoning and rational ideas inscribed in various institutions.[50] He stresses that such reasoning and ideas garner a particular lifestyle conducive to the capitalist order. He notes an elective affinity between Calvinist beliefs and the economic ethics of modern capitalism. In other words, Weber spotlights the connection between the rationalization of economic life and irrational value commitments. In doing so, he notes the coevolution of economic rationality with other forms of social organization.[51] Economic ideas are embedded in locally specific contexts, and they evolve. Ideas shape particular types of social projects, and the new realities created by such projects affect economic practices, which in turn affect economic ideas.[52]

When do new ideas evolve and trigger particular social projects? The concept of "the new spirit of capitalism,"[53] explored by Luc Boltanski and Ève Chiapello and adopted in this book, seeks to capture the transformative moment that details when and how capitalism requests a different spirit of its participants. The operational logic of capitalism, or capital accumulation as an end in itself, is detached from the moral sphere. However, individuals and societies need reasons and justifications to be committed to capital accumulation. In other words, a change in the capital accumulation mechanism requires a new spirit to justify the new mechanism, and capitalism needs to mobilize external resources available at a given moment to formulate a new spirit. This explains why the spirit of capitalism is "inscribed in the cultural context in which it is developing" and is "imbued with cultural products that are contemporaneous with it."[54]

Boltanski and Chiapello thus elucidate that a new spirit of capitalism emerged from the critiques of capitalism. During the peak of Fordist economies in the Western countries in the 1960s, laborers, intellectuals, and students demanded more human elements and autonomy under the machinelike work organization. Meanwhile, the capital accumulation mechanism began to shift from mass production to varied and differentiated productions, alongside developments in networks, finance, and technology.[55] The capacity of laborers to synthesize personal traits and skills to create products has been emphasized as industries have generated more and more profits by creating added value from certain qualities of human beings.

At this critical juncture, capitalism drew on a set of discourses about creativity, autonomy, and flexibility, which was adapted from its critique, to formulate a new spirit to guide how to engage in work. The demand for humanized capitalism led firms to develop personalized capitalistic production and self-regulation. Firms emphasized more flexibility and less hierarchy as new desirable features of the workplace and demanded that the laborer become an enterprise that runs self-autonomously.[56] The laborer was expected to synthesize the whole personhood to create added value. In other words, one had to "invest" in the self to generate "profit."[57] The new capital accumulation by "more personal matters of competence" gave birth to new notions of work, self-worth, and ethics, all of which advocated personal responsibility.[58] The current capitalism demands entrepreneurial subjectivity, or the enterprising self, from its participants as a disposition where one regards the self as a risk-taking and self-responsible agency. By adapting its critiques as its new spirit, capitalism liberalized the workings of corporations rather than liberated workers from the machine-like work organization.

Creativity has become the new spirit of post-Fordist cities. Jim Mc-Guigan argues that numerous policies concerning creativity, notably a creative city, demonstrate the permeation of the new spirit or the enterprising self in the forms of economic manuals, political objectives, and lifestyle models in cities.[59] Likewise, I approach the enterprising self as the new spirit of rapidly liberalized and deregulated Seoul, as an ethos whereby one regards the self as an agency, imposing self-organization and self-responsibility not only on economic undertakings but also on lifestyle at large. Thus, I explore the ways in which people in Seoul internalize and negotiate the enterprising self in their own contexts. Therefore, I examine both subjectification as a type of disciplinary practice and as social control under neoliberal regimes[60] as well as the workings of self-reflexivity toward such a socialization force.[61]

From Hongdae Natives to Ethical Entrepreneurs

Hongdae's popularity spread with its cafés, reached a climax with its clubs, and subsequently returned to its cafés as its main scene. The city government announced plans to create the Hongdae Cultural District (HCD) just as Hongdae's popularity peaked in the early 2000s. The announcement of the HCD project prompted local cultural workers and artists to mobilize. People from dance clubs formed the Club Culture Association (CCA) at the end of 2003. Soon after, people from other domains, such as live clubs and art, design, and performance spheres, established the

Hongdae Culture and Arts Cooperation (HCAC) in early 2004. Members of both organizations participated in CD policy preparation and the feasibility review in 2004. In this sense, the policy plan triggered new socialization processes even before its actual implementation.

Both the CCA and the HCAC asserted themselves as legitimate stakeholders and confronted each other over what constituted Hongdae culture. People from the dance clubs presented themselves as "prosumers" who possess capabilities to upgrade Hongdae culture befitting a postindustrial society.[62] Indeed, they saw Hongdae culture as esoteric, anachronistic, and elitist. In contrast, HCAC members accused the CCA of being doctrinaire, profit-driven, and uncreative. People from the non-dance-club sectors defined themselves as "Hongdae natives" who were safeguarding the original Hongdae culture.[63]

Significantly, both groups created polarizing self-images—the protectionist identity (natives) and the reformist identity (prosumers)—drawn from the same set of policy ideas. Although the point of contention was the identity of Hongdae culture, the conflict emerged in the context of debates on how to make sense of the economic and cultural value embedded in Hongdae culture.

Hongdae clubs, shops, and cafés gave birth to new cultural forms and provided life space to people who desired to pursue new lifestyles; clubs, shops, and cafés became the markers of Hongdae culture, as their makers infused artistic ingenuity, skills, sensibilities, work ethics, and life ethos into their creations. These performed and objectified makers' traits, skills, and values constitute Hongdae-ness. When consumers discern Hongdae-ness, they become place connoisseurs.[64] Hongdae-ness is thus something to be performed and evaluated.

Hongdae-ness is also good business. It is the competitive edge that distinguishes Hongdae clubs from nightclubs, products made in Hongdae from mass-produced items, and artisan coffee from franchise coffee. It creates new value that stimulates the formation of new markets, notably real estate and tourism. Hongdae-ness oscillates between self-expression (the art of objectifying the self) and exchange value. Accordingly, makers can become artists, artisans, and entrepreneurs. Hongdae culture is created by the coeval processes of subjectification and objectification. The HCD policy announcement pinned down these processes of being and becoming into "recommended cultural facilities and businesses forms"— or objects of policy implementation.[65]

Despite the positive feasibility review, in 2005 the city and district governments postponed the HCD project indefinitely because of issues concerning legal compatibility. In short, the HCD project was canceled. Bewildered, the two opposing groups, the CCA and the HCAC, gathered to contemplate their experiences with the policy project and to envision Hongdae's future. The participants talked about the need for the commercialization of Hongdae culture and market success to ensure its continuation. For the continuation of Hongdae culture, the participants said that they should perform the role of "intermediaries."[66] I argue that the unexecuted Hongdae project offered a new occasion through which people contemplated a new challenge: how a good culture can make a good business.

Since the policy cancelation, Hongdae has been in decline, with gentrification noted as the main cause. I have revisited the former representatives and key members of the HCAC and the CCA repeatedly for over a decade. Significantly, while these organizations have long been inactive, their former members have been occupied with discussions of work, labor, and capitalism. I have also visited the representative of the Hongdae-ap Culture and Art Social Cooperation (HCASC), a new local organization established in 2014. He refused to associate the organization's identity with the label "artists" and asserted that its members should instead be seen as "laborers."[67] Ever since the introduction of the CD plan, new self-images—Hongdae natives, prosumers, intermediaries, and laborers—have emerged.

Policy does not necessarily produce expected results. Rather, it triggers ongoing social changes. It provides a social language through which participants self-reflect, explain their situations, and create social relations.[68] Conversely, newly emerged meanings and relations challenge the values and meanings attached to a given project. The HCD as a set of ideas provided resourceful and argumentative logics through which people reconfigured citizen subjectivities. A shift from symbiosis between culture and economy to problematizing the self affected a series of subjectification processes. I argue that policy cancelation, ironically, better elucidates the performative capacity of policy ideas and the coevolution of ideas and the self.

I also contemplate the growing voice about ethics that bother my interlocutors. I have interviewed the same people for over ten years. They are concerned with labor and capitalism. Have they already internalized the notion of the enterprising self? Or are they now developing a new form of corrective critique to the current urbanism? They are not sanguine about the revival of Hongdae culture. However, they all recognize that they are living in a new era of capitalism and are struggling to come to terms with its spirit. This raises the question of whether becoming an entrepreneurial

Seoulite, despite its display of the internalization of the new capitalistic order in post-Fordist Seoul, also highlights a new form of corrective critique to living in the current order.

This book looks into Hongdae-ness and examines how people interpret, adapt, and perform the new spirit of capitalism in post-financial-crisis Korea. Chapter 1 spotlights the controversies surrounding Hongdae culture. To what extent are typical urban amenities such as clubs, shops, and cafés the markers of Hongdae culture? This chapter explores the relationship between markers of Hongdae culture and its makers. Hongdae culture is complete when the objectification of Hongdae-ness takes place and when consumers, in turn, discern the objectified and performed Hongdae-ness. In this case, where is the thin line between the cultural and the commercial drawn?

Chapter 2 unpacks the HCD project. It documents the paradigm shift in Korean cultural policy and the coexistence of cultural exceptionalism and market reasoning in the cultural policy known as the cultural district. It then examines the intertwined vocabularies of cultural critiques and management in the Hongdae place-marketing report, which provided the set of rationales to create a cultural precinct in Hongdae. This chapter thus unveils how a new spirit of the enterprising self became inscribed in the Hongdae project.

Chapter 3 traces how cultural workers and artists in Hongdae strategically utilized policy ideas to convey their criticisms of the status quo and to harness their position as legitimate stakeholders. These participants were segregated into two groups—namely, the CCA and the HCAC. This chapter details the reconfiguration of self-presentation and the mobilization of social relations provoked by the HCD policy project.

Chapter 4 explores the ongoing socialization processes in the aftermath of the cancelation of the HCD policy project. Policy cancelation motivated the creation of a new local forum known as the Hongdae Culture Academy in 2006. Its participants proposed to envision themselves as cultural intermediaries who produce, market, circulate, and sell cultural products. This chapter thus juxtaposes the citizens' roles articulated in the Hongdae place-marketing report with the self-presentation of the new intermediary and highlights their similarities. The chapter analyzes the extent to which the policy experiences brought about new realities in Hongdae, even though the CD plan was not executed.

Chapter 5 continues to examine the ongoing social changes, which include the establishment of the HCASC and the emerging voices concerned with good businesses and ethics. It probes how people who have been working in Hongdae since the 1990s struggle to live with the current capitalist environment as they perceive it. The chapter therefore explores the historicity of the subjectification processes.

The conclusion revisits a theme that has emerged repeatedly: To what extent does Hongdae represent the present-day lifestyle of Seoulites? What does it mean when people in Hongdae have begun to talk about how to make a living rather than how to make culture? The conclusion thus contemplates the significance of Hongdae culture in understanding post-financial-crisis urbanism in Seoul.

1

Fluid Hongdae Culture

> Hongik University Area [Hongdae] is a free-spirited neighborhood
> bursting with places to enjoy unique culture. On the streets one may
> find amateur bands playing by the road and busy merchants catering
> to customers at a flea market. Tucked away in the alleys are small-
> scale art galleries and independent venues displaying the works of
> young artists in the area. At night, clubbers can routinely be seen
> waiting in long lines around Hongdae's clubbing area. Also, the
> streets are always a parade of colorful clothing, as this is also where
> to spot some of Korea's most unique fashionistas.
> —Flyer with Mapo district's guide to the Hongdae area, 2015

The usual urban consumption places such as clubs, shops, street stalls, and
cafés have been regarded as representative of Hongdae culture. Yet these
are typical consumption places that can be found in any city. How and
why have such places become the markers of Hongdae culture? What is
Hongdae culture? This chapter answers these questions by examining the
controversies surrounding Hongdae culture.

Markers and Makers of Hongdae Culture

Hongdae is the area surrounding Hongik University in Mapo district located in the middle western part of Seoul (see Figure 1).[1] It is a mixed locale comprising residential areas, schools, and commercial facilities. In
general, images, ambiance, sounds, and tastes produced in Hongdae—in
other words, typical local scenes—have been regarded as representative of

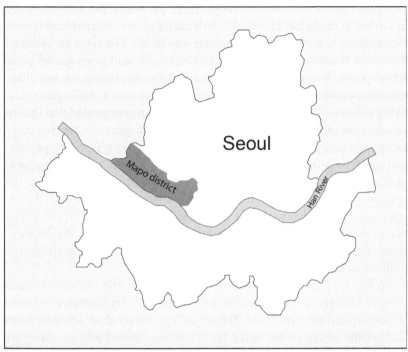

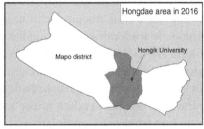

Figure 1. Expansion of the Hongdae area within the Mapo district of Seoul, 2000 to 2016. *Data sources:* Seoul Metropolitan Government, "Tosichŏngbo: Chidosŏbitsu" [City information: Map service], http://gis.seoul.go.kr/SeoulGis/ Naver/MetroInfo.jsp?tr_code=metroinfo; Yŏngju Han et al., *Wŏltŭkŏp chŏllyakchiyŏk changsomak'et'ing: Hongdaejiyŏk munhwahwalsŏnghwa pangan* [Place marketing of the (2002) World Cup strategic areas: Schemes for vitalizing culture in Hongdae] (Seoul: Seoul Development Institute, 2000); Sooah Kim, "Hongdae konggan ŭi munhwajŏk ŭimi pyŏnhwa: Konggan iyongjaŭi kiŏkŭl chungsimŭro" [Changes in the cultural meaning of the Hongdae place: Focused on the memories of place users], *Midiŏ, Chendŏ wa Munhwa* [Media, Gender, and Culture] 30, no. 4 (2015): 83–123; Hongdae Cultural Studies Network and Seokyo Arts Experiment Center, *Hongdaeap munhwayesul saengt'aegye hwalsŏnghwarŭl wihan chŏngch'aekyŏn'gugwaje* [A study of the policy for the activation of the culture and art ecosystem in Hongdae area] (Seoul: Seoul Foundation for Arts and Culture, 2014).

Hongdae culture. Its liberal atmosphere, in particular, has been observed as unique to Hongdae. In contrast with the flamboyant Gangnam lifestyle, Hongdae style represents a bohemian way of life.[2] In 2000 an architect described Hongdae as an "artistic, eccentric, chic and avant-garde" place where people become "free."[3] In 2006 a designer wrote that she met "like-minded people in Hongdae, who want to trudge and wobble rather than living in haste."[4] More recently, a Japanese Korean commented that she felt comfortable only in Hongdae. In her words, Hongdae was where acceptance and openness toward diversity and individuality was well respected.[5] Currently, both the city and the district governments promote Hongdae as "a free-spirited neighborhood."[6] However, Hongdae is also seen as the epitome of gentrified urban neighborhoods. Hongdae has expanded from 0.66 square kilometer to some 3 to 4 square kilometers over the last fifteen years (see Figures 1, 2, and 3).[7] This expansion has prompted the displacement of residents and businesses from Hongdae and their resettlement to outlying neighborhoods.

Hongdae's current atmosphere was birthed in the mid-1960s when Hongik University established an art college, and art institutes began to cluster around the university. The art college attracted art students from all over the country who opted for a relatively liberal private university instead of a national school.[8] The art academies were renowned for cultivating successful students who could enter Korea's famous art colleges. These art academies gave Hongdae the reputation of being the cradle for future artists. Indeed, Hongdae has benefited from the liberal and artistic atmosphere created by the students enrolled in the college and academies.[9] In the early 1990s, Hongdae became a notable subcultural and countercultural area. Its independent music scene in particular received significant attention from critics, scholars, and the press.[10]

Various media and scholarly reports on Hongdae culture had been produced extensively between the 1990s and the early 2000s in tandem with the flourishing of cultural studies in Korea. Themes such as soap operas, Internet cafés, and hair coloring occupied studies on everyday life in Korea and expanded the boundaries of cultural studies in the 1990s. Recent studies on Hongdae have started to pay attention to its different periods of development.[11] The 1990s are regarded as the foundational phase when cultural agencies, such as students, artists, and cultural workers, began to congregate in Hongdae. The 2000s are depicted as the diversification phase when cultural movements, urban consumption, and government-led tourism concurrently prospered.[12] The period from 2010 on is portrayed as the phase when investment capital surged into real estate markets in

Figure 2. The front entrance
of Hongik University in 2004.
The university's main gate
was under construction.
(Photo by the author.)

Figure 3. The front entrance of Hongik University in 2016, with the completed
main gate. (Photo by the author.)

Hongdae, and entertainment companies tightened their monopoly of music production. This most recent phase of development has led some people to remark that "Hongdae has already perished."[13]

Despite worsening conditions for cultural production in Hongdae, diverse topics ranging from emerging cultural forms to restaurant reviews and stories of successful start-ups have been widely published in the last ten years.[14] Clubs, cafés, performance venues, street stalls, and shops in Hongdae have been constantly referred to as places that display the characteristics of Hongdae culture and Hongdae style. The city's official website presents Hongdae as a major hotspot for "Korean club culture," where all the latest music genres can be experienced, and Hongdae clubs as the places where the passion of the Seoul's young people explodes.[15]

Scholars have observed how economic restructuring and employment changes caused by deindustrialization and the concurrent rise of culture industries spark vibrancy in cities.[16] Notably, the formation of urban enterprises in the inner-city areas, stimulated by local geographical contingencies (i.e., human, social, spatial, and industrial resources in a locality), is seen as the trigger of multifunctional spaces that in turn invigorates property markets and the new economy.[17] These explanations account to some extent for the development of Hongdae.

In 2000 residential homes less than four stories (which were built before the 1980s) made up almost 90 percent of the houses in Hongdae and provided students, artists, and cultural workers with affordable living and working spaces.[18] The basements and first stories of these low-rise houses were used as studios, ateliers, clubs, and offices (see Figures 4 and 5). The availability of such spaces contributed to the dense social networks that facilitated crossover cultural genres and new businesses.[19] Moreover, expanded subway lines have connected Hongdae to Seoul's digital and media industry clusters, the surrounding metropolitan regions, and the international airport.[20]

Gradually, some districts in Hongdae have been transformed from residential zones to quasi-commercial zones. The change in land usage thus stimulated local real estate markets. In 2014, 280 real estate agencies were registered in Hongdae.[21] Likewise, the number of accommodations for international tourists increased rapidly in recent years. In 2015 Hongdae boasted 158 guesthouses, which constituted more than 90 percent of guesthouses in the Mapo district.[22] Meanwhile, the number of restaurants, food stands, pubs, and bars within a one-kilometer radius from the Hongdae Tourist Office was reported as 1,544.[23] In 2014 the number of fashion-related shops was reported as 350,[24] and in 2013 the number of cafés was reported as approximately 530.[25]

This place attribute-focused perspective, which explains the relationship between socioeconomic restructuring and the formation of cultural milieus, cannot entirely explain the development of Hongdae's scene, however. This chapter thus endeavors to unveil the workings of value in

Figure 4. A low-rise multiuse building, 2009. (Photo by the author.)

the making of the Hongdae scene. Dean MacCannell argues that tourist hangouts often reveal the way sites and information conjoin to become attractions in particular temporal and spatial settings.[26] This coupling process is deeply affected by collective experiences and social conditions. Similarly, the case of Hongdae demonstrates how commercial places have become the markers of culture embedded in particular local settings.

By putting forward that Hongdae culture has always been associated with commercial places, the following discussion examines the formation of markers of Hongdae culture. How and why have commercial places been regarded as representative of Hongdae culture? What does this reveal about Hongdae culture?

Figure 5. A café on the first floor of a house, 2016. (Photo by the author.)

Live Clubs and Dance Clubs

The opening of a punk club called Drug in 1994 consolidated Hongdae's status as the place for independent and alternative culture. In the 1990s, musicians, filmmakers, and artists who resisted repressive state censorship, apprenticeship-based production, and genre-exclusive production flocked to Hongdae to pursue alternative interests.

Live band performance first emerged in the clubs within the American army bases located in Seoul after the Korean War. Subsequently, live music became popular in the 1970s, when those people who experienced neither the Japanese colonial regime nor the Korean War sought to advance youth culture. A number of momentous events took place in the 1960s. The labor- and student-led April 19, 1960, revolution overthrew the autocratic first president, Rhee Syng Man (1948–1960). In the following year, however, Park Jung Hee (1963–1979) and his allies led a military coup. In 1964 Park's military regime normalized diplomatic relationships with Japan amid nationwide protests. Koreans saw the restored relationship as a national humiliation; it would erase the Japanese colonial invasion of Korea (1910–1945). Those teenagers who witnessed the democratic revolution, military coup, and nationalistic movements in the 1960s reached their twenties in the 1970s—in other words, they came of age to lead new cultural movements.[27] In particular, they led the folk music scene, which was characterized as live, amateur music performances.[28] Many of the folk musicians were university students, and some of them sang about social irregularities. In reaction to this youth culture, Park's military government strengthened media censorship and enacted various legislations including "performance legislation," "fire legislation," and "public hygienic legislation."[29] The censorship deterred free expression while the new legislations restricted live music performance. Additionally, the development of broadcasting services and dissemination of household TV sets proliferated the production of recorded music.[30] By the end of the 1970s, the live music scene in Korea had significantly languished, although it continued in the underground scene during the 1980s.[31]

Beginning in the 1990s, bands started gathering in Hongdae to perform live music, especially punk and rock music.[32] Following the founding of Drug, similar clubs such as Freebird, Jammers, Rolling Stones, and Spangle appeared in 1996.[33] These live clubs attracted numerous bands that played mainly punk and rock music. The clubs developed what became known as the underground and independent music scene. The press, cultural critics, and scholars displayed great interest in the live clubs and featured them as the hub of an alternative and independent culture.

A massive infrastructure failure in 1994 indirectly contributed to the formation of Hongdae's independent music scene. Seongsu Bridge, one of the bridges over the Han River, collapsed because of a fault in the suspension structure. With the bridge closed, Seoulites experienced poor surface traffic conditions between the northern and the southern parts of the city for three years. This physical detachment stimulated the congregation of people in Hongdae, who opted to stay in the northern part of Seoul rather than make a detour to Gangnam in southern Seoul.[34]

Toward the end of 1996, a punk music performance known as the Street Punk Show further publicized Hongdae as a subcultural area.[35] That same year, a music festival of independent bands was held in Hongdae for the first time, and Drug made its own label and produced its first album.[36] In 1997 Open Club Union was established as the first union of live clubs. In 1999 its members, who held concurrent positions as scholars, cultural critics, and NGO members, campaigned for the creation of legal terms to institutionalize live clubs as venues for music performance rather than as entertainment businesses. They succeeded in legitimizing live clubs as performance venues. In 2004 Open Club Union became the Live Music Cultural Development Association and was accredited by the Ministry of Culture and Tourism. In 2004 it was reported that twenty-two live clubs operated in Hongdae.[37]

Since the 2000s, however, the live club scene has turned sluggish. Some clubs have even folded because of financial difficulties. Meanwhile, dance clubs where DJs played the music became popular in Hongdae. A club culture emerged with the opening of dance clubs such as Sangsoodo, M.I., Jokerred, and Hodge Podge in 1995. Subsequently, Underground and Hooper appeared in 1996; Whangkeom Toogu (Golden Mask), Matmata, and Saab in 1997; and 101, 108, Hiranya, and Nbinb in 1999.[38] Foreigners, university students, young professionals engaged in culture-related businesses, and Koreans who had returned from their overseas studies were all attracted to these clubs. Artists and cultural workers also started to gather at the clubs.[39]

Initially, two different types of dance clubs—namely, techno clubs and dance clubs—emerged in Hongdae. The techno clubs featured techno music while dance clubs provided places where people could dance to music of various genres. Techno, the latest music genre at that time, was considered rather difficult to dance to, therefore, hip-hop and standard dance music replaced techno music, and the distinction between techno clubs and dance clubs became insignificant.

In 2002 the dance clubs based in Hongdae accounted for approximately 72 percent of all dance clubs in Seoul.[40] In 2004 the number of dance clubs located in Hongdae was reported as twenty-eight. The success of Hongdae's Club Day contributed to the widespread popularity of club culture.[41] Started in 2001 with "Clubber's Harmony" as its slogan, Club Day was a unique program that allowed visitors to enter all affiliated clubs with a single ticket. Club Day occurred every fourth Friday of the month and soon attracted as many as ten thousand visitors on some Fridays. Club Day had a unique management scheme that split the revenue generated by entrance fees evenly among the affiliated clubs. This plan was seen as an "idealistic strategy" aimed to help small-sized and specialized clubs based on egalitarian and unionized operation principles.[42]

As Hongdae dance clubs became widely popular in the early 2000s, those engaged in the live club culture emphasized that having fun in the dance clubs should be seen as different from performing and appreciating music in the live clubs. As Choi, owner of Club Jammers, told me, "Here [a live club] is for appreciating performance, and there [a dance club] is for dancing, enjoying, and relieving stress."[43] Kim, manager of Soundholic, explained, "Well, live clubs and dance clubs are differentiated. Live clubs are closer to small theaters rather than places for play culture."[44]

These differentiated descriptions of live clubs and dance clubs can be observed in the newspapers and magazines published in the same period:[45]

> As the hegemony of club culture has gone to dance clubs, there appeared concerned voices. Contrary to live clubs that produce experimental creativity, dance clubs are regarded as places for fun and dancing, which led Hongdae culture to become entertainment culture.[46]

Based on a dichotomous framework—playing live music versus dancing, performance versus having fun, and culture versus entertainment—the dance clubs were criticized for causing the excessive commercialization of Hongdae culture.

However, another perspective asserted that dance clubs offered new subcultural forms.[47] Clubbers and DJs were seen as performers in the sense that clubbers express their feelings and sentiments toward DJs who, in turn, observe clubbers' dancing and play their music according to clubbers' performance.[48] The communication and interaction between clubbers and DJs was thus perceived as a form of meaning making. Furthermore, Hongdae dance clubs were seen as creating new cultural content by integrating art, music, and performance.[49]

It should be noted that Hongdae dance clubs were distinct from the existing nightclubs. To some people, Hongdae dance clubs offered an alternative for those who did not like the nightclubs.[50] The Seoul city government's commissioned report, *Place Marketing of the [2002] World Cup Strategic Areas: Schemes for Vitalizing Culture in Hongdae*, describes nightclubs as commercial facilities pursuing profits. In contrast, the report notes, Hongdae dance clubs are places where people with cultural sensitivities and tastes visit to appreciate dancing and music.[51] During my field research between 2003 and 2006, I observed that my interlocutors perceived the differences between Hongdae dance clubs and nightclubs in terms of the types of visitors and their socialization patterns, dress codes, dancing styles, the venues' music genres, and interior designs. For example, in 2003 a female office worker who visited Hongdae dance clubs for the first time, said, "It is strange. People are dressed differently. The atmosphere is different. People here [at one of the most popular Hongdae clubs at the time] appear to me that they think very differently from others."[52]

Faced with criticisms for diluting Hongdae culture, dance clubs began to implement self-regulation by controlling visitors and their conduct. For example, in 2004 I observed one of the clubs with a signboard stating, "We sincerely apologize, but due to many previous bad experiences, G.I.s are no longer permitted to enter Hongdae Clubs." At that time, American soldiers were not allowed to enter the clubs, as they were often involved with drugs and debauchery. In 2005 Hongdae dance clubs also displayed posters that prohibited unacceptable behavior such as jaywalking, fighting, littering, and the excessive expression of affection in public spaces.[53]

While Hongdae live clubs differentiated themselves from dance clubs, dance clubs also distinguished themselves from nightclubs. Both live clubs and dance clubs associated fun and entertainment with commercial places yet emphasized they were not commercial places. Both reiterated that their staff and visitors were makers and performers of cultural content rather than suppliers and consumers of amenities and services. Indeed, the emphasis on "doing" the club scene rather than consuming club venues created added value for Hongdae clubs. This added value turned clubs into the markers of independent and alternative music and club culture. Doing the club scene made Hongdae clubs different from others and thus substantiated their unique identity, which also created marketplace competence. In other words, the unique identity became a value-added label, which in turn increased the exchange value of Hongdae clubs in the club market.

Hongdae clubs thus became the markers of performance embedded in the conceptual demarcation between the commercial (consumption) and the cultural (creation). However, this definition of Hongdae clubs is difficult to translate into institutional terms. Although Hongdae clubs were widely promoted as the sites of cultural tourism, they were not institutionally acknowledged as cultural venues. For example, the city government promoted clubbing in Hongdae as a unique cultural experience in Seoul during the 2002 World Cup. It featured Hongdae clubs as one of the best cultural sites in Seoul and even designed tour bus service called Culture Tour Bus for visitors to attend the various Hongdae dance clubs during the tournament period.[54] However, clubs and club-related programs such as

Club Day, Sound Day, Road Club Festival, and Live Club Fest were not featured in the cultural and tourist map for Hongdae created for the 2002 World Cup.[55]

Furthermore, dance clubs in Hongdae were technically illegal because of the absence of appropriate legal terms. As the dance club venues were too small to be registered as dance halls under the category of entertainment businesses, these clubs could only be registered as standard restaurant businesses. Yet restaurants were governed by a different set of regulations and taxation from entertainment businesses. According to the food and hygiene legislation, dancing in restaurants violates public health laws. Hongdae dance clubs demanded the revision of the laws while authorities occasionally cracked down on Hongdae dance clubs. In 2016 the Ministry of Food and Drug Safety tightened the enforcement of public health legislation. For two decades, the dance clubs' controversial status highlighted the ambiguity of demarcating the cultural and the commercial.

The current Hongdae club scene is not as vigorous as it once was. Its heyday back in the mid-1990s to mid-2000s coincided with the period when the K-pop industry solidified new systems of talent production, talent training, and market management.[56] The rapid growth of entertainment houses such as JYP, SM, and YG led to the concentration of people, networks, and infrastructures in a handful of enterprises.[57] Musicians who were based in Hongdae since the 1990s pinpoint that independent musicians faced difficulties in presenting and selling their music amid the growing K-pop industry.[58] The former CCA representative commented to me that Hongdae dance clubs in the late 1990s and early 2000s magnetized hip-hop musicians, rappers, DJs, and dancers; the entertainment house YG, based in Hongdae since 1996, has benefited greatly from the congregation of people in Hongdae clubs.[59] A musician further commented that currently Hongdae clubs might serve as shelters for temporal sojourners who wish to be recruited by the monopolistic entertainment enterprises.[60]

Street Stalls and Shops

Street hawkers used to line up along the playground across from the main gate of Hongik University beginning in the late 1990s. These sellers occupied the streets and lit up small lamps in the night to sell their handicrafts. One of them, Chŏng, told me, "It was so beautiful. Everybody lit candles because of the lack of electricity. Many photographers came here to take photos, and people in buses and cars often got off just to take photos. Later, outsiders came, and commercial zones appeared all along [the streets]."[61]

A scholar observed in 2000 that some teenagers who just met in a club began to sell their handmade accessories in order to pay for their drinks on that day.[62] A street hawker in 2004 remembered that artists started creating street stalls by bringing their artwork to the area.[63] Although these artists infringed on public order and hygiene regulations, their colorful artwork, clothes, and glittering lamps created an illuminating view: "6 p.m. in front of the playground facing the University, young street hawkers are setting up their stands. They are selling colorful accessories and clothes made by them. They are one of the creators who made the unique Hongdae fashion."[64]

Over time, more and more people came to the area to sell various fashion items and handicrafts. Street hawkers often stressed that their products were unique: the street hawkers and their friends had crafted them or flew overseas to countries such as Japan, Italy, and India to handpick the items personally.[65] Flea markets also appeared in Hongdae. The Free Market, which started in 2002, for example, has become a regular weekend event. The Free Market emphasizes its artistic creativity:

> The Freemarket, a spontaneous Arts market and festival, has suggested the new culture space, which breaks down the border between creators and citizens. Since the opening of the first market in June 2002, the walls of life vs art and the curtains of artists and citizens were lowered by allowing anyone to participate by becoming a creator, a consumer, a Free-player, or as a volunteer.
>
> Creators can participate as a seller and culture creator. People who do not create can enjoy and broaden their culture experience. The Freemarket also acts as a stimulus for people, who can create but were afraid alone, can now become a creator. Any individual can become a part of the market.[66]

In principle, people could sell their handmade products at the market on the condition that they registered as "member artists" of the Free Market. However, some street hawkers complained that the membership registration limited their businesses. One street seller wanted to sell her handmade accessories every day, and therefore she did not join the Free Market because the event takes place only on Saturdays. However, she clarified that even though she was not a member artist, her products were not "market products" but "handmade products."[67] Another seller also said that the Free Market treated nonmembers' products as "mass-produced market products"[68] even though the sellers had handcrafted these products. The media also reported that street hawkers were copying the artists' products and turning the area into a commercial zone: "Free Market started from sincerity. It was the same to artists and visitors, something like a family atmosphere. But this place has been changing to a commercial zone, when street hawkers began to sell products here."[69]

A market product in Hongdae refers to an item that is mass-produced for mass consumption, hence lacking the aesthetics and tastes of makers and merchandisers. Moreover, a market product is considered lacking uniqueness and is not Hongdae-like. Another street hawker said that she had to make everything by herself because people "here," referring to Hongdae, were looking for something "unique."[70] Based on interview data from street hawkers, I observed that the main difference between sellers "here" and sellers "there" (in non-Hongdae areas) was whether sellers had the artistic taste and skills to make products by themselves. An interlocutor showed me a name card holder crafted from plastic chewing gum packaging (see Figure 6). Although my informant was not a street hawker, this name card holder, which he referred to as "something nice,"[71] seems to exemplify the artistic taste, craftsmanship, and uniqueness that people expected from things "made in Hongdae."

In the early 2000s, some of the small shops in Hongdae had their own designers who produced their own brands. Also, there were networks of people who provided items and services only for insiders. As Hong, a band singer, explained to me, "My friends took me to some people who make the 'one and only' hairdo or clothes. . . . This kind of thing happens

Figure 6. A name card holder made from plastic packaging, 2004. (Photo by the author.)

only through connections. In fact, these people are producing real unique cultures."[72] The street hawkers in Hongdae had to craft artistic items in order to appeal to visitors and customers, both of whom expected unique products. While this certainly limited the choices of items sold by street hawkers, being artistic served as an effective business strategy.

Now, however, it is difficult to find street hawkers because the local association of businesspeople controls the operation of street stalls (see Figures 7 and 8). Nonetheless, the rapport between Hongdae and its makers' craftsmanship and artistic taste has been preserved to some extent. Shopping in Hongdae is still promoted as experiencing the "stylish stores directly managed by independent fashion designers."[73] Hongdae-ness created by craftspeople-cum-street hawkers has continued to inspire the establishment of craft shops, workshops-cum-shops (referring to workshops that make and sell handmade products), and secondhand shops. According to the local magazine *Street H*, some of the owners of cafés, shops, restaurants, and workshops regard their businesses as involving the creation of new things, tastes, and communities where people interact and meet—rather than mere commercial activities.[74] For them, their businesses represent the means to achieve financial autonomy as well as to realize their desired lifestyles. Running a business is thus seen as the realization of the self: one who makes good products, creates good places, and leads a good life.

The representative of a waste-wood recycling workshop observes that people often find handwork therapeutic, as they aspire to be engaged in humanized production processes to nurture the self rather than indulge in consumption.[75] A café owner shares that he regards himself as one of the many artists in Hongdae because running a café is akin to creating his

Figure 7. Independent street hawker in front of the playground in Hongdae, 2004. (Photo by the author.)

Figure 8. Street stalls controlled by area business associations in front of the playground in Hongdae, 2016. (Photo by the author.)

own artwork—one that embodies original content and labor.[76] An owner of a workshop-cum-store reveals that what makes her job pleasurable is her neighbors' visits to her shop for idle chitchat; her handmade products turn business encounters into occasions for cozy interactions.[77]

Running a small business in Hongdae is tough. The steep rent is especially burdensome. Even though Hongdae has become a heavily commercialized area, it remains one of the few places in Seoul where various cultural infrastructures, businesses, and encounters with diverse peoples converge. Some shop owners remark that they are not seeking wealth but an autonomous life by selling the fruit of their labor and creating an environment where they can live with people who appreciate their tastes and products. Interestingly, those who emphasize that their businesses afford them the means to realize their selves, lead an autonomous life, and create communities note that they came to Hongdae to pursue those same values.[78] Hongdae-ness, inspired by craftsmanship as self-modeling, has also objectified a self-image for those who create not only products but also the places where they work. For some people, handmade products, self-designed workspaces, and self-employment symbolize autonomy and individuality.

Cafés

Several cafés in Hongdae started hosting ad-hoc live performances and concerts in the late 1980s. They were regarded as the birthplace of Hongdae culture:

> Cafés and clubs such as Electronic Café, AlloAllo, Baljunso [Power plant], Space Ozone [located in Jongno area of Seoul], and Gompangee [Mold] are places where the "furious kids" were active in the late 80s and the early 90s. These furious kids produced provocative and avant-garde projects, exhibitions, plays, and performances in the cafés and clubs. However, only their names remain now. These places were the incubators of recent diverse cultures and arts.[79]

The 1990s were characterized by the emergence of new cafés with peculiar architectural design. These cafés offered distinctive management concepts and services such as fortune-telling services and free local telephone calls. They also hosted exhibitions and performances and sold art books and crafts. The term "Hongdae café" was therefore established as a genre of urban amenities. The early 2000s saw the emergence of another type of café dubbed "multicultural cafés," which facilitated diverse cultural events, parties, and exhibitions.[80] Ko, a café manager who used to run the legendary clubs Baljunso and Myeongwolgwan in Hongdae, remarked to me that people who enjoyed Hongdae's atmosphere in the 1990s came to appreciate "quality" in the 2000s: "When people were younger, back in their twenties, they didn't have enough money in their pockets. . . . Now that they have aged and hold professional jobs, they want good quality, even though they still want to feel like they are back in their twenties."[81]

Quality does not necessarily mean extravagance. Based on the interviews that I conducted and information I gathered from the media, quality refers to the tastes, aesthetics, and efforts committed in preparing handmade coffee and food as well as the maintenance of a space that offers both privacy and sociability to customers. Coffee makers are seen as "technicians" because they are experts and professionals who possess the knowledge, technology, and skills to make proper coffee and craft café space.[82] This virtuous act of coffee making is a value-added practice.

These Hongdae cafés have created a standard for Hongdae style. This style includes characteristics such as being located in a residential area; the availability of customized coffee making, terrace seats, and commu-

Figure 9. Café B-hind, a well-known Hongdae café, popu-larized by its owners in their book, *Shall We Open a Café?* (2005). (Photo by the author.)

nity tables; the playing of particular genres of music; and the composition of the café space (see Figure 9). Interestingly, Hongdae style initially emerged in the domain of fashion, in close affinity with the club scene. Hongdae style was regarded as one of the trendiest fashions and was followed closely by those in the fashion industry, advertisement agencies, and journalism: "The commercial area in front of Hongik University, which is called Café Street or Orange Street, is changing into a new fashion plaza of the new generation."[83] One newspaper reported, "In the department store, she [a salesperson] says, 'It is called club casual, since this style looks much like what university students are wearing at the clubs in the Hongdae area.'"[84]

Today, Hongdae style has evolved to include not only the particular ambiances of cafés, shops, and restaurants but also particular types of people:

According to the survey done by a matchmaking company, single men and women prefer "Gangnam style," followed by Itaewon style and Hongdae style. Both men and women prefer Gangnam style for similar reasons. Roughly speaking, they pointed to the glamorous appearance, polished fashion, and fat purse for their preference of Gangnam style. What then distinguishes Gangnam style from Hongdae style? The fancy appearance and polished outlook? Hongdae style is not flashy and polished but aspiring to individuality. . . . All in all, Hongdae style is the opposite of Gangnam style.[85]

Hongdae culture has been the source of inspiration for the pursuit of quality. The evolution of Hongdae cafés has continued; multicultural cafés in the 2000s were seen as having directly inherited the Hongdae culture of the 1980s:

It is not accidental that the multicultural cafés run by artists who used to work in Hongdae area have emerged here. At the end of the 1980s, there already existed multicultural places for exhibition, play, dance, and performance, and they . . . led to club culture, movie culture, and party culture. As shown, multicultural cafés inherited Hongdae culture.[86]

Recently, the number of cafés in Hongdae has increased significantly. A tourist pamphlet published in 2016 states, "Hongdae culture = café culture," and features a map of Hongdae's "Café Streets."[87] Another guidebook published by the district government emphasizes the craftsmanship of coffee and introduces Hongdae cafés as cultural places.[88] Some cafés are labeled "art cafés" and "multicultural venues" because they are seen as functioning as exhibition places, theaters, studios and workshops, clinics, publishers, and art institutions:[89]

Built along the quiet alleyways of Hapjeong-dong and Sangsu-dong, the Café Street areas are filled with specialty cafés that offer hand-drip and fresh home-roasted coffees, as opposed to large coffee franchises. There are also numerous one-of-a-kind cafés with distinctive personalities, such as book cafés operated by publishers, or those that offer live music and performances. Some cafés here also serve as cultural salons where literary readings, performances, exhibitions or even flea markets are held.[90]

Going to a café in Hongdae is not just about grabbing something to drink. A café in Hongdae must serve delicious coffee. Cafés here are places for work and rest but also for exhibitions and sometimes even bazaars.[91]

Similar types of cafés have sprung up in increasing numbers. Indeed, there must be compelling reasons for people to run cafés in Hongdae despite the steep rent and intense business competition. Similar to the reasons people want to open shops in Hongdae, new café owners highlight pull factors that include the existing cultural infrastructures; established local culture and historicity; and the diversity of the people who work, live, and visit the locale. For some cafés that aspire to become multicultural venues, the community of like-minded people who share tastes and sensibilities is regarded as crucial to the creation of new café content.

For example, those cafés labeled "art cafés" endeavor to build cafés as places where cultural and industrial content are integrated to create something new.[92] Such art cafés are used as venues for book editing, theater performance, exhibition, pottery making, music recording, group studying and learning, medical treatment, and filmmaking. These cafés create places where people can paint, sing, write, dance, and make friends and meet neighbors. In this respect, the makers of art cafés are seen as cocreating new cultural content and communities with café visitors and users.

The sense of artistic ingenuity is materialized in the forms of self-designed cafés, handmade furniture, and fastidious coffee-making processes. Some café owners explain that cafés are the media where diverse cultures are communicated and shared.[93] Tastes, skills, and attitudes are embedded in both the coffee and the café. Certainly, not all cafés in Hongdae are art cafés or multicultural cafés, and not all café owners are artists, performers, crafters, or technicians. Yet some people regard running cafés as creating place, fostering community, and living one's desired lifestyle. For them, running a café is a value-driven practice. In the words of one café owner, his café is "beyond just a café."[94]

In Between the Cultural and the Commercial

Are clubs, shops, and cafés the markers of Hongdae culture or are they the cause of its commodification? Hongdae clubs gave birth to the independent music and club scene and provided the labor to produce K-pop. While dancing in the Hongdae clubs is illegal, clubbing in Hongdae has been globally publicized as a must-do to experience Seoul's contemporary culture. The mushrooming of shops and cafés has been blamed for the excessive commercialization of Hongdae, which turned the area into an insipid consumption district. However, these shops and cafés are also the places where people aspire to create new things and tastes and pursue new work ethics and lifestyles. Where is the line drawn between cultural and commercial Hongdae?

Perhaps clubs, shops, and cafés become the markers of Hongdae culture when their makers objectify their values. In other words, it is the makers who perform Hongdae-ness. Musicians, DJs, street hawkers, merchandisers, coffee makers, and shopkeepers concretize Hongdae-ness via materializing their sense of individuality, autonomy, and artistic ingenuity in the form of clubs, shops, and cafés. Those who can appreciate Hongdae-ness distinguish Hongdae clubs from nightclubs, handcrafted items from mass-produced items, and artisan coffee from franchise coffee. When visitors and customers discern the makers' artisanship, aesthetics, work ethics, and tastes as objectified in a place, they become place connoisseurs and Hongdae people.

Hongdae-ness represents the quality that makers strive to objectify. Hongdae-ness is distinct from mainstream culture, market products, franchise shops, standardized menus, and depersonalized places. Hongdae quality equals value and is associated with resistance against standardization and deindividualization; it is closely linked to the values of freedom and individuality. People emphasize craftsmanship and creativity as a way of expressing and constructing an autonomous self. Quality is thus achieved when people have attained a projected self-image. Quality is something to be envisaged, performed, attained, and evaluated. Performing Hongdae culture is, to a certain extent, quality management and self-regulation.

Hongdae-ness is also good business.[95] Quality as market distinctiveness distinguishes Hongdae clubs, shops, and cafés from others, therefore creating new value in various markets. Hongdae-ness is both a commodity and its exchange value: Hongdae culture at large is thus a commodity under the continuous process of value making. This conversion of resources into commodities—including those that have not always been treated as commodities—is seen as the "core procedure of capitalism."[96] Such interconvertibility incorporates virtually everything into monetized exchange and organizes the intersection of structures via monetized exchange.[97] When Hongdae culture emerged as a new cultural phenomenon, it was associated with alternativeness, freedom, diversity, idiosyncrasy, and youthfulness. Indeed, Hongdae culture denoted the new generation and their sensibilities and the liberalized society and its increased tolerance for individuality. At the same time, it also entailed the sophistication of consumer capitalism. Images, sounds, tastes, and atmospheres that were regarded as representative of Hongdae culture developed into products labeled as Hongdae style.

How should Hongdae culture be promoted when it comprises both cultural value, which ought to be protected from commodification, as well as economic value, which accords a product its competitive edge? Where should the line be drawn that demarcates the cultural and the commercial, or value as priceless and value as price?[98] This issue of the duality of value or the "core procedure of capitalism" penetrates Hongdae-ness. Oscillating between self-expression and marker of distinction, fluid Hongdae-ness turns clubs, shops, and cafés into the markers of Hongdae culture as well as the markers of commodification. Accordingly, the makers of such places can be artists and artisans or entrepreneurs. Hongdae culture, understood in this way, represents more than the lifestyle associated with clubbing and coffee. Instead, it reveals the coeval process of subjectification and objectification.

2

Fluid Cultural Policy

The 2002 World Cup was regarded as an immense opportunity for Korea to rebuild its staggering economy and international standing after the 1997 Asian financial crisis.[1] The national government came under the twin pressures of economic crisis as well as the nation's democratic reform. Since the collapse of the military state in 1987, civil and social movements had asserted the rights of individuals as idealized, liberal citizens emancipated from the repressive state.[2] During this time, culture emerged as the national soul, as well as a new engine of the national economy.

The Seoul city government employed the slogan "culture World Cup, civic World Cup, and environmental World Cup" in its promotion of Seoul as a world-class city.[3] Appropriate measures that could enhance the unique images of Seoul were sought. The city government commissioned its research institution, the SDI, to embark on the project of promoting the city. One strategy that the SDI recommended in its report, *Place Marketing of the [2002] World Cup Strategic Areas: Schemes for Vitalizing Culture in Hongdae*, was to create a cultural district in Hongdae. This chapter scrutinizes the policy ideas embedded in the project of making the HCD.

The place-marketing report approaches Hongdae as the site of endogenous local culture that embodies the potential to lead the proposed public-private partnership initiative:

> Among the strategic areas, this study focuses on a place agglomerated with cultural facilities and businesses, possessing significant cultural potential to lead to the culture of Seoul and facilitating endogenous movements for local cultural development. Through the study of such a place, we aim to propose an efficient model for the cooperation between the public and the private sectors.[4]

The place-marketing report is the first municipal document that treats subculture as an object of cultural administration. Since its publication, the terms "Hongdae," "Hongdae culture," and "Hongdae people" have appeared in a series of municipal vision and planning reports. Indeed, Hongdae is featured in Seoul's world-class city vision plan for 2006 and beyond,[5] while independent culture appears as constitutive of one of the Seoul-style businesses, which comprise finance, culture, multimedia, and fashion industries.[6] Likewise, the district government believed local artists and cultural workers in Hongdae would advance the information technology industry and boost the local economy.[7] Overall, these administrative documents approach Hongdae culture as a source of urban vibrancy and an incubator to produce human resources for the urban industries.

The city and district governments soon encountered the conundrum of translating Hongdae-ness into existing policy language. Incorporating Hongdae culture into formal cultural policy required redefining cultural spaces. For example, the announcement of the HCD plan provoked a heated debate on whether dance clubs should be seen as cultural or commercial places. Furthermore, the announcement prompted local cultural workers and artists previously marginalized in city administration to come to the fore of urban politics. Some welcomed the plan because policy execution would counteract excessive commercialization. Others criticized the plan for its potential to induce real estate bubbles that might displace cultural workers and artists from Hongdae.

Policy practice does not necessarily produce expected results. Rather, it generates ongoing social changes. Policy provides people with a context for mobilizing social meanings, relations, and organizations.[8] Through policy language, policy participants self-reflect, explain the status quo, and engage with other actors.[9] Conversely, newly emerged social meanings, relations, and organizations challenge the values and meanings attached to the given project. In particular, cultural policy marks the site where "the clash of ideas, institutional struggles, and power relations in the production and circulation of symbolic meanings" take place.[10] Therefore, the politics surrounding a cultural policy often take place implicitly via the confrontation of meanings. A certain set of values and meanings can be mobilized as effective resources to incorporate economic and social benefits. This chapter thus explores the issues of who defines values and meanings and based on what grounds.

What kinds of value should count in the making of the cultural district in Hongdae, when Hongdae culture is regarded as constitutive of both immeasurable and nonmarketable cultural value to be protected from market reasoning and economic value to be turned into a world-famous cultural product? The following discussion examines the core rationales that justify cultural intervention and permeate the Hongdae policy project.

Korean Cultural Policy: Between Cultural Value and Economic Value

Culture is generally regarded as constitutive of all the aspects of human activity.[11] In the context of cultural policy, however, this general definition is not feasible because it would encompass all aspects of policy making.[12] Because of its administrative purposes, cultural policy confines culture to a certain sector in order to draw up administrative boundaries. Accordingly, when relevant authorities set new administrative tasks in the cultural sector, the process of redefining culture takes place at the level of institutional discourse. The definition of culture is thus temporary and flexible. Indeed, culture is not clearly defined in Korean legislation.[13] However, the administrative boundaries of Korean cultural policy have continuously expanded to include spheres as diverse as the population's well-being, environmental issues, and the content industry—the latter referring to products containing information in the form of letters, images, and sounds.[14] Currently, Korean cultural policy is widely referred to as a "department store of policies."[15]

The national government did not prioritize culture as a core state issue immediately after the Korean War. In fact, the government began to implement so-called traditional cultural policy only in the 1960s, with significant focus on anticommunism, modernization, and nationalism.[16] Traditional cultural policy emphasized culture as "pure public good," "good for [the] soul," and as "civilizing."[17] In the early 1970s, the authorities became aware of the importance of culture, especially its civilizing and publicity effects. Confronted with Korea's rapid industrialization and the consequent erosion of traditional values, the authorities saw the promotion of traditional culture as the solution to stem the disintegration of traditional values. Consequently, the Culture and Arts Promotion Act was adopted in 1972 and enforced in the following year.

In accordance with the act, state cultural administration was established in the 1970s. Public funds were channeled to provide subsidies to artists as well as organizations such as the Korean Film Council (1973) and Korean Arts and Culture Education Service (1974). The distribution of public funds focused on assisting creatorship and had remained so for the next forty years.[18] The act categorizes culture and arts together under the broad theme of literature, art, music, theatrical entertainment, and publishing. This definition signified a change in the government's approach to culture: it provided a broader definition than the previous understanding of culture, which referred primarily to traditions and heritage.[19] However, cultural policy during the 1970s heavily advocated governmental ideologies of national prosperity. The government regarded cultural policy as a means to boost concerted economic campaigns and modernization efforts. One scholar aptly described state cultural policy during this period as the "publicity department of a developmental state."[20]

During the 1980s, state cultural policy pursued the full-scale democratization of culture. Ironically, the term "democracy" was not allowed in political, economic, and social policies under the military regimes. Only official cultural policy publicized democracy because cultural democracy reflected state efforts to establish and expand a cultural infrastructure and its relevant agencies at the national level.[21] Because of the changing lifestyles that resulted from Korea's economic prosperity, the government began to pay attention to sports, tourism, and leisure. It also adjusted its policy targets to focus on consumers beyond artists and heritage holders. The increased state intervention in mass culture, however, grew alongside the intensification of censorship by the authorities.

The 1980s also witnessed the intensification of the political democratization movement, which eventually ushered in a direct presidential election system in 1987 and subsequently prompted a series of state administration reform. In the realm of cultural administration reform, the newly established Ministry of Culture was tasked in 1990 with advocating national progress via the enhancement of quality of life and cultural welfare. In 1992 a new law known as the Culture Industry Promotion Act was enforced.[22] The implementation of a new cultural planning strategy in 1993 proclaimed a shift in cultural administration principles from regulation to autonomy, from centralization to regionalization, from creatorship to consumers and industries, from anticommunism to national unification, and from nationalism to globalization.[23]

Together, these new legislations and institutions promoted culture in order to liberate citizens from totalitarian and autocratic ideologies and practices attached to the previous military regimes. Evidently, the objective of cultural policy at that time was to oppose totalitarian subjectivity and to undo the function of culture under the previous dictatorial regime. The new government asserted culture as an avenue to invigorate individual autonomy from the repressive systems and regulations. Thus, the new regime's cultural policy paid significant attention to public arts and mass culture as resistant forces against authoritarian ruling elites and also shed new light on the culture industry as an avenue to elevate mass culture. Meanwhile, international pressure on globalization and treaties for free trade also prompted the Korean government to focus on the culture industry as a strategic national industry.[24] Under such circumstances, Korea's cultural policy began to embrace leftist notions as well as nationalistic ones to promote both liberalistic civil society and exports.

This blend of leftist and nationalistic approaches to culture and the culture industry heightened after the 1997 financial crisis. In 1998 the former leader of the democratization movement, Kim Dae Jung, became the fifteenth president of Korea. Kim's government had the urgent task to abrogate the IMF bailout, which the public regarded as loss of national sovereignty and hence a national disgrace.[25] Previously, military regimes had utilized economic crises to suppress labor and enforce governmental policies. Civilian regimes, however, were under pressure to reform the state-planned and developmental economy toward a more liberal one.[26]

Consequently, Kim's government effected a series of reforms to steer the role of the government from regulation toward one of governance. The government conducted the IMF's programs, which centered on economic liberalization—that is, trade liberalization and deregulation of the financial and labor markets.[27] Governmental technocrats adopted the requirements of the IMF as a pragmatic process to advance economic restructuring.[28] The civic sectors pursued the vision of less state intervention and more individual freedom regarding economic restructuring as inevitable.[29] Kim's administrative principle, known as the "co-development of democracy and market economy," summarizes the direction of such reforms.[30] Layoffs and contingent employment, together with schemes concerning employability, rehabilitation, flexibility, and self-entrepreneurship, were implemented as crisis management.[31] In particular, the government pursued the development of knowledge-oriented industries and supported start-ups and rehabilitation efforts.

Amid the context of crisis management, culture emerged as a source of national development and pride. This cultural turn was accelerated by the unexpected popularity of Korean dramas across Asia. The Korean broadcasting industries were badly affected by the financial crisis. Advertising sales, the main income sources of broadcasting companies, plummeted as a result of austerity measures taken by client companies. Between 1997 and

1998, the three biggest broadcasting companies in Korea lost almost 28 percent of their incomes from advertising sales. Currency depreciation further burdened broadcasting companies in their purchase of foreign products—a common problem for broadcasting companies across Asia, with the exception of Japan. Thus, Korean broadcasting companies began to pay attention to the export of programs—notably, television programs—to other struggling Asian neighbors. This turned out to be mutually beneficial. From the late 1990s to the early 2000s, the price of Korean dramas was approximately one-tenth that of Japanese dramas.[32] The demand for cheaper products thus led to the unexpected success of Korean broadcast programs in Asia, a phenomenon that came to be known as K-wave.

K-wave's immense popularity strengthened the status of the culture industry as the vanguard of Korea's knowledge-oriented industries. Likewise, the market success of cultural products was regarded as proof of cultural autonomy against globalization. Amid the IMF bailout, the sense of economic crisis and cultural crisis became fused. In addition to Korean society's anxiety about lagging behind developed economies and being overtaken by emerging ones, globalization stimulated concerns about the preservation of authentic national culture.[33] Under such global and national circumstances, Korean cultural identity was asserted for solidifying both its national identity and national economy:

> The global and homogenous pattern of cultural consumption and consequent change in national sentiment can confuse national cultural identity, which contributes toward the construction of a nation-state. . . .
> Establishing cultural identity for the content of the cultural industry should be taken seriously. The cultural industry is becoming a dominant culture as the structures of cultural field change and their influence on the receivers is becoming significant. To be successful in international markets, strengthening the competitiveness of the Korean cultural identity is an urgent task.[34]

The culture industry is understood as a domain where authenticity—referring to immeasurable cultural value—would produce higher value-added goods, thereby strengthening their competitive edge in global markets.[35] The proliferation of the culture industry would foster both economic and cultural autonomy. Such reasoning prompted state cultural policy to articulate economic vocabularies and those of cultural resistance concomitantly.

The importance of culture in envisioning the revival of the national economy has been intertwined with the discourse on creativity. In 2005 the Ministry of Culture and Tourism presented "C-Korea 2010," a midterm plan widely perceived as an ongoing embodiment of the state cultural administration principles in Korea's cultural policy.[36] The plan aims to elevate Korea as a leading nation of the creative economy through the promotion of the "3Cs—culture, content, and creativity."[37] Culture represents the key to competitiveness in the global era; content, referring to the content industry, is interpreted as the necessary breakthrough for overcoming slow growth; and creativity is regarded as an engine for national development in the twenty-first century.[38] Under this state vision of the three Cs, cultural policy aims to shape—at least discursively—the socioeconomic development of the nation:

> Culture and arts compose the core value of creativity and diversity, which will lead future national competitiveness. The importance of creativity and diversity penetrates the core of socioeconomic development that we put emphasis on. They [creativity and diversity] are not necessarily for the sake of arts or personal satisfaction. They are the sources of all the aspects of our development.[39]

During Lee Myung Bak's presidency (2008–2013), the term "culture industry" was replaced with "content industry" in state cultural policy. This implies that Lee's government shifted its focus to the strategic management of the content industry as the main objective of state cultural administration.[40] Accordingly, policies concerning the content industry have become departmentalized into specific domains such as the character industry, the animation industry, the cartoon industry, the game industry, the craft industry, the sports industry, the intellectual property industry, the K-wave, and the design industry.

With such departmentalization, cultural policy has become less associated with the liberalistic connotation underpinning the promotion of individuality and autonomy. Instead, cultural policy has advanced so-called entrepreneurial socialization aimed to transform "culture to K-Wave content, the academia to content production bases, universities to training centers for content industry laborers, young people to idol-entrepreneurs, the press and media to a state marketing and publicity department, and regional governments to K-Wave enterprises."[41]

Fluid CD Policy: Between Market Failures and Marketization

In 2000, as Seoul prepared to host the 2002 World Cup, the SDI place-marketing report noted Hongdae's significance in showcasing the contemporary culture and lifestyles of Seoul. It proposed to introduce Hongdae culture to foreign visitors and to promote local cultural businesses by creating a cultural precinct. Given that the CD policy was enacted in 2000, the proposal clearly had that new cultural policy in mind.

The CD policy was issued as a new decree under the Culture and Arts Promotion Act. Disorganized development of Insadong area in Seoul stimulated the design of the CD policy. Insadong used to be a tranquil gallery area located near one of the royal palaces in central Seoul. However, street hawkers and megastores displaced the small-scale art shops, galleries, and traditional restaurants in the locale and were criticized for ushering in uncontrolled commercialization. In response, governmental intervention to restrict the sprawling businesses was requested. The Ministry of Culture and Tourism commissioned the Korea Culture Policy Institute (KCPI) to formulate a new cultural policy to preserve places with rich cultural assets from the effects of rapid urban development.

The CD policy designates places with high density of cultural resources, distinguished cultural identity, and geographical and administrative territories as cultural districts.[42] Cultural resources may include nature, religion and beliefs, science and arts, unique modes of living, political and military buildings, and unique industries.[43] With such a broad definition, virtually anything in a locality can be regarded as a cultural resource.[44] Under the CD policy, recommended local cultural businesses and facilities may receive tax reductions, low-interest loans, public relations and marketing support, environmental improvement subsidies, and aid for developing cultural programs and local committees. Additionally, land and building usage within the designated district can be restricted for the sake of promoting recommended businesses and facilities. The CD policy has been implemented in Insadong (2002) and Daehangno (2004) in Seoul, Heyri (2009) in Paju, Open Port (2010) in Incheon, and Jeoji (2010) in Jeju.[45]

The CD policy was initially designed to complement the existing cultural policy, which focused on subsidizing individual artists and institutions.[46] It thus marked a shift in the focus of Korean cultural policy from heritage to the management of cultural resources, including places. The act did not specify the operational details of the CD policy; the purposes and scope of its implementation thus depended on the initiatives of the local authorities. In Insadong, the CD policy was implemented to preserve local cultural resources. Meanwhile, the policy was effected in Daehangno to forge a cultural cluster where production, distribution, consumption, and education of performing arts are seamlessly interconnected.[47]

Interestingly, the objective of the CD policy remains ambiguous. Indeed, it can be interpreted as an intervention to regulate the workings of market rules based on cultural exceptionalism and also as a policy that regards culture as part of economic activities. For example, the KCPI explains that the CD policy aims to protect the noneconomic and historical values of urban spaces from market forces:

> The city spaces that accommodate noneconomic and historical values but lack competitiveness are often ignored. It is due to the market-economy system based on capitalism, efficiency, and rationality. . . . But the cultural district, which values meanings, could overcome the limitation of the market system.[48]

This statement reiterates that cultural value should not be evaluated by the market rationality and that state intervention in the form of the CD policy is necessary.

In another report, however, the KCPI states that the CD policy could enhance the promotion of the culture industries and the economy:

> The local governments endeavor to construct a cultural infrastructure aimed at transforming a site of history and tradition to that of cultural production and consumption. . . . The projects such as the "cultural street" and the "cultural district" . . . would contribute to promoting culture and arts, the culture industry, and further boost the economy.[49]

Both rationales—one stressing that culture should transcend economic evaluation and the other urging governments to support the economic valorization of cultural value—justify the CD policy as governmental intervention.

In addition, the CD policy is embedded in the obscure legal definition of "cultural facilities." The act does not clearly identify culture, rather, it defines "arts and culture" together as established genres of arts, such as performing arts, fine art, and traditional music.[50] Cultural facilities are thus legally defined as the places where activities related to established artistic genres take place.[51] The term "cultural facilities" is crucial for the execution of the CD policy because it determines what is to be authorized as components of a cultural district. This problematizes the enforcement of the CD policy in an area where new forms of culture emerge as local culture. Indeed, the case of Hongdae—with its clubs, restaurants, and cafés that prompted the emergence of independent culture, café culture, and club culture—poses new challenges to the CD policy.

The CD policy can be seen as a scheme to utilize and manage cultural resources for place making. This renders the CD policy similar to cultural planning. The latter emerged in the early 1990s in North America, Australia, and Europe and refers to an urban strategy to utilize cultural resources for solving problems arising from deindustrialization in cities.[52] Cultural planning defines cultural resources broadly to include arts and media, sports and recreation, heritage, public spaces, and local industries.[53] To administer such a wide range of cultural resources, cultural planning emphasizes interdisciplinary policy practice so that policy participants can synthesize different types of knowledge and forge partnerships among diverse stakeholders.[54]

Furthermore, cultural planning can be seen as an extension of the creative city thesis, which has been adopted globally as an urban development strategy to promote culture-led urban development. The notion of the creative city emerged in the late 1980s when a new approach toward organizational and managerial thoughts and practices was necessary to cope with complex urban issues arising from deindustrialization.[55] Beginning in the early 2000s, Richard Florida's notion of a creative city,[56] which further emphasizes human resources for urban growth, has been translated into strong advocacy for an appropriate environment where workforces engaged in knowledge-based industries work, live, and play. The creative city thesis has generated significant repercussions in cultural and urban administration globally. As one such attempt at postindustrial city development, Korea's CD policy demonstrates how regional governments incorporate city-based cultural planning into cultural policy initiatives to utilize cultural resources for urban management.

Fluid HCD Project: Between Cultural Politics and Entrepreneurialism

Although the making of a special precinct in Hongdae was proposed with the 2002 World Cup in mind, the actual project was not implemented

in time for the tournament. Instead, the city government promoted Hongdae clubs during the World Cup by operating a hop-on bus service for
visitors to Hongdae clubs.[57] Later in 2003, the city government announced the possible implementation of the CD policy in Hongdae. The
decision was partially stimulated by the increased popularity of Hongdae
clubs among both domestic and international visitors. Immediately after
the announcement, the district office commissioned the Hongdae Environmental Development Institution (HEDI) to conduct a year-long policy feasibility review. The relevant review and administrative plan were
completed in 2004. A series of events occurred in Hongdae during this
preparation period: local artists and cultural workers protested skyrocketing rental prices, a record number of people visited the area, and two
local organizations—namely, the CCA and the HCAC—were established.

The Hongdae place-marketing report is crucial to the understanding
of the context in which local events, as well as the reconfiguration of social
relations, unfolded. The report provides the resourceful discourses and
argumentative logics for people to interpret the status quo and to engage
themselves in the policy project. The task force organized to craft the
place-marketing report included a number of researchers from the SDI, a
civic activist previously engaged in labor and environmental activism, and
a cultural program planner based in Hongdae who pioneered the local
techno club scene. This task force can be seen as a form of public-private
partnership. Interestingly, some of the contributors who shaped the place-
marketing report subsequently established the CCA and the HCAC and
also participated in authoring the policy's feasibility review. The feasibility
review cited the place-marketing report extensively, especially those sec-
tions concerning the rationale for making the cultural district in Hongdae
and selecting recommended cultural businesses and facilities. The engagement of the same participants in producing a series of reports and their
overlapping content thus demonstrate the significance of the Hongdae
place-marketing report in concretizing the policy project.

The place-marketing report paid attention to the emergence of new
buildings, the influx of franchise businesses and amenities, and escalating
rental rates that displaced small-scale subcultural facilities and businesses
from Hongdae. Although the term "gentrification" was not widely used at
that time, the report in fact documents incipient gentrification. The report
utilizes various terms—including youth culture, club culture, underground, independent, nonmainstream, multicultural space, and cultural
diversity—to explain the cultural value of Hongdae and the need for governmental intervention.

For example, the report spotlights the independent cultural scene as the source of "the spirit of freedom and punk, which drives resistance against dominant social systems and regulations and produces creative and productive culture."[58] It recommends legalizing the dance club business to foster the cultural rights of young people who enjoy music and dancing in Hongdae clubs:

> Young people who like music and dancing are now deprived of their right to enjoy. It is also pointed out that the closing down of more and more clubs, due to the crackdown on them, tarnishes the charm of Hongdae. Therefore, there is a great necessity for "the legalization of techno clubs" and "the recognition of the club space as the cultural space."[59]

Why does the report pay particular attention to dance clubs? Strictly speaking, many dance clubs conducted their businesses illegally because of the absence of appropriate legislation. Registered as restaurant businesses yet allowing people to dance, these clubs were in fact violating public order and health legislations. Claiming their clubs were cultural venues rather than restaurants or entertainment establishments, dance club owners petitioned the city government to authorize dance clubs as cultural businesses. The place-marketing report highlights this legality issue as an impetus to promote endogenous and bottom-up cultural movements. It explains why "techno" should be regarded as a legitimate cultural genre and why club businesses should be legalized. For example, the report states that musicians and DJs are experts with their advanced electronic musical instruments; the clubs facilitate a community where free-spirited professionals and artists can pursue alternativeness and create both cultural forms and social movements for peace and respect.[60]

Significantly, governmental intervention aimed at fostering the spirit of freedom, the rights to culture, and the endogeneity of culture was packaged as holistic place-marketing strategies. The report defines place-marketing as "a new strategy that applies marketing skills of business administration to urban regeneration" so that a locality should be reinterpreted and reidentified as the "objects, targets, means, and subjects of marketing."[61] It highlights the clear assignment of responsibilities to each marketing agent and the collaboration across agents as critical for successful place-marketing and local governance.[62]

Under such a framework, Hongdae was reidentified as a district with marketing places, products, and agents. Its stadiums, youth subculture spaces, multicultural spaces, and consumption spaces were identified as "marketing places"; its cultural businesses, facilities, events, festivals, independent culture, techno culture, art culture, cultural facilities, and food and attractions were identified as "marketing products"; its cultural workers, businesspeople, residents, and district authorities were identified as "marketing agents."[63]

The techno club, for example, was expected to become a globally competitive product and was to forge an urban cluster to drive cultural and technological innovation:

> Techno clubs clustered in Hongdae are a magnet that attracts foreigners and a space where human resources from various domains meet and form new communities. They possess the potential to make a futuristic cultural space suitable for the era of information and digital technology, to develop Korean-style techno culture, and to advance a global cultural tourism product.[64]

Place-marketing efforts were equated with "cultural politics" that resist the "penetration of a spatial mechanism of capitalistic logics."[65] The report highlights the displacement of artists and cultural workers due to rent increases as a major problem in Hongdae. By framing Hongdae and its residents in the language of marketing and business management, however, the report turns Hongdae into a marketplace, cultural activism into market activities, and urbanites into marketing agents. Overall, the report treats cultural politics as a countermeasure to the market forces in the contours of place marketing.

The place-marketing report further indicates that Hongdae lacked the human networks to manage the abundant human resources available in the locale. Human resource networking is seen as a prerequisite for effective place marketing. Consequently, "cultural subjects" are encouraged to identify themselves as "place imagineers" and "cultural engineers," equipped with futuristic imagination and hands-on capabilities to create "culture" and "places."[66] Thus the report elucidates not only how to manage cultural resources and urban space but also how to nurture self-organizing agencies. A desirable resident of Hongdae is envisaged as one who plays the multiple roles of marketing agent, place imagineer, and cultural engineer.

As I observe in the introduction, the generally liberal task force members adopted marketing frameworks to address critiques of capitalism and cultural politics, and I interpret this apparent incongruity as "culture jamming."[67] In summary, the report reframes urban governance as place marketing and merges the notions of cultural politics, entrepreneurialism, and active citizenship. It treats culture as a medium through which people obtain a stakeholder identity, thereby internalizing self-organization as a new urban management technique.

Achieving Symbiosis of Culture and Economy

This chapter explores the core rationale—that culture should transcend market rules by achieving market competence—embedded in the trio of Korea's cultural policy, CD policy, and Hongdae place-marketing report. How, then, does culture acquire market competence? Seen either as an embodiment of an entity or of authenticity, culture distinguishes one from the other, thereby creating added value and enhancing market competence. Cultural policy should thus intervene to protect cultural identity or authenticity so that cultural products, as the embodiment of authenticity, can be sold in the market. This would enable culture to survive by gaining market competitiveness and obtaining its autonomy. Simply put, market competitiveness is a prerequisite to cultural autonomy.

Cultural politics as a critique to capitalism asserts resistance against the standardization and commodification of human beings under the rationalistic workings of capitalism. It highlights identity as the essence of a being and asserts intervention in protecting cultural identity under the threats of market forces and globalization. On the one hand, governments address this critique to justify intervention in the cultural sector by illuminating the contribution of culture to the public interests. On the other hand, culture as a source of the creative economy enables the national economy to gain a competitive edge in global markets. In this respect, cultural leftism, nationalism, and active citizenship are all combined to justify state cultural policy.

How Hongdae-ness should be translated into the existing policy language so that cultural administration can effectively foster a liberal spirit in public culture as well as transmit it to urban sociality and economic creativity thus poses a conundrum for city and district governments. The place-marketing report advocates a discursive solution to achieve these dual objectives. First, it valorizes the cultural value of dance clubs, thereby presenting club culture as a Korean-style club culture and clubs as "proper" cultural places. As such, clubs need (cultural) intervention to protect them from market rules. Second, it valorizes the economic value of the clubs as potential world-famous cultural tourism products with added value: a Korean-style club culture. In this case, (economic) intervention is needed to boost the market for clubs.

The Hongdae place-marketing report shares the generic ideas that the creative city thesis advocates: the success of a city (or a place) hinges on the people's creativity, and therefore a city should foster the enabling environments where human creativity is transmitted to urban milieus and economies.[68] The report also demonstrates the dual approach to culture—that is, culture as value to be protected from commodification and culture as commodities with exchange value. It amalgamates the vocabularies of cultural politics and those of business management, which result in equating cultural politics with the transcendence of market rules via becoming marketing agents. This leads to the problematization of the self rather than tackling the duality of value that penetrates the pursuit of the symbiosis of culture and economy. Cultural workers and artists are thus encouraged to perceive their dispositions, work outcomes, workspaces, residences, and sociality as marketing products. By marketing such target objects successfully, they can keep their work and living space away from the threat of capitalistic logics. This combination of cultural politics and business management became the policy language that underpinned the HCD project, in which its future stakeholders needed to explain Hongdac-ness and present themselves accordingly.

3

Becoming Prosumers and Natives

> In the past, we had the romantic idea that we were creating
> something, although we were poor. Now, it seems that we are getting
> into a different situation in which capital plays a role.
> —Cho (representative of HCAC), interview by the author,
>   Seoul, October 12, 2004

When the Seoul city government announced its plan to create the HCD in 2003, news reports highlighted the plan's potential to promote diverse cultural businesses through the formation of a cluster of clubs, unique cafés, and galleries.[1] In tandem with the city government's announcement, people from the Hongdae dance clubs established the CCA in November 2003. Shortly thereafter, people from other sectors—including those engaged in the live clubs, arts, design, performing arts, and cultural programming—established the HCAC in February 2004. The CCA and the HCAC exchanged sharp debates about whether the dance clubs should be cultural or commercial places. The former argued that the dance clubs were cultural places essential to the emergence of new forms of culture and economy. The latter asserted that original Hongdae culture, tarnished and commercialized by the proliferation of dance clubs, should be restored.

In general, debates and conflicts reveal the norms and structures that underpin local society as well as provide indicators of social change.[2] Conflict does not indicate any rigid state of deadlock but instead highlights a transformative and dynamic state in which communicative interactions take place. In a cultural policy project, conflict appears as the clash of ideas, and resolving conflict takes the form of negotiating and creating certain definitions and meanings.

The contrast between the CCA's and the HCAC's conceptualizations of the dance clubs as cultural or commercial places, respectively, reveals the ambiguities embedded in the Hongdae project. How should people present themselves as legitimate stakeholders of the project when the authorities concomitantly assert the economic valorization of cultural value for market expansion and the protection of cultural value from market forces? While Chapter 2 examines the resourceful discourses and argumentative logics embedded in the Hongdae project, this chapter explores the extent to which such discourses and logics served as the language for policy participants to self-reflect, articulate their situations, and engage other actors.

Are Dance Clubs Cultural Places?

When the Hongdae place-marketing report acknowledged club culture as part of Hongdae culture, questions regarding just how cultured are dance clubs began to permeate local debates. Some people opined that the report coined the term "club culture" for the sake of legitimizing dance clubs as legal businesses.[3] Overall, those who did not acknowledge dance clubs as cultural places understood Hongdae within the framework of the confrontation between "cultured us" versus "commercial dance clubs." As Kim, a manager of a live club, told me, "Unfortunately, Hongdae, which attracted mania groups, is getting so much popularity due to the dance clubs. It is becoming a flirting place for the young."[4] A 2004 post to an HCAC Internet bulletin board (which is no longer available) said, "Against the clubs! . . . I think the clubs at present are rather similar to alcohol and dance houses, which are only striving for money. They are not cultural places."

Those who saw the dance clubs as mere commercial places regarded the clubs as the main cause for Hongdae's commercialization, skyrocketing rental rates, displacement of cultural workers and artists, and the consequent dilution of Hongdae culture. Such sentiments were especially pronounced when Club Day attracted a record-breaking number of visitors during 2003 and 2004. Club Day was sponsored by the big marketing budgets of Korea Tobacco and Ginseng Corporation, British American Tobacco, and Motorola, among many others.[5] These sponsorships increased the criticisms of the dance clubs.

In 2000 the dance clubs began to unite to challenge the illegality of the dance club business. At first, the Space Culture Centre, an NGO concerned with community making, began to coordinate the dance clubs' efforts.

This NGO, together with the club managers and owners, appealed to city authorities. However, the city government had no authority to handle the issue. The Ministry of Health and Welfare oversees food and hygienic legislation, which in turn regulates requirements and conditions for restaurants, dance halls, and entertainment establishments. The dance clubs had to devise other ways to publicize club culture as "culture proper." The Club Day initiative began in March 2001, and the monthly event became a tremendous success in generating revenue and publicity. Lee, a member of the Space Culture Center and also a coauthor of the Hongdae place-marketing report, published several academic writings about club culture. He defines club culture as a branch of youth subculture originating from the club space: "Club is defined as *a multi-cultural space with unique music, dance, people and communication*. And club cultures are defined as the unique youth subcultures, which are generated, shared and changed around the club space."[6]

In addition to publicity campaigns, the dance clubs also submitted petitions to the Ministry of Culture and Tourism.[7] The 2002 petition stated that the dance clubs created a new culture that should be protected in order to make Seoul a cultural city: "Club culture is forming a new local culture and community. . . . [C]lub culture is certainly a new type of culture, which should be protected in order to construct Seoul as a cultural city."[8]

Given the legal complexity, the dance clubs also suggested creating a special precinct in Hongdae where legal exemptions could be made for certain cultural facilities and businesses. This proposal was very similar to the Hongdae place-marketing report recommendations. Indeed, as two members from the Space Culture Center participated in the writing of the place-marketing report, it is highly likely that the dance clubs' interest was reflected in that report.

Choi, the representative of the Space Culture Center, commented to me that people from outside the dance club sector remained entrenched in their "old-mannered way of doing culture, staying in their ateliers and overlooking the relationship between production, consumption, and circulation."[9] The dance clubs, according to Choi, had the potential to construct a self-sufficient economic system by integrating production with consumption. He argued that the dance clubs provided spaces where people became cultural and economic producers, thereby co-performing club culture and co-operating the club businesses. Choi opined that the dance clubs could thus nurture new cultural forms, social relations, and economic activities.

Choi basically emphasized a new perspective on understanding the relationship between culture and economy. However, people outside the dance club sectors found his framework of old Hongdae versus new Hongdae offensive. The announcement of the CD project heightened the existing uneasiness about the dance clubs among the non-dance-club people, who became concerned whether the dance clubs would be recommended as cultural facilities for the project. The local conflict over the dance clubs reflects fundamental questions surrounding Hongdae culture. Where should the line delineating the cultural and the commercial be drawn? How should one make sense of the economic value and the cultural value embedded in Hongdae culture?

Becoming Prosumers

As the number of dance clubs increased, the Space Culture Center and the dance club owners established the CCA to undertake tasks related only to the dance clubs.[10] Since its establishment in 2003, the CCA sought to legalize the dance club business, publicize club culture, and operate club-related events—all of these in addition to managing Club Day. In 2005 the CCA defined itself as a networking communicator on its website (which is no longer available):

> Club Culture Association is managing and sponsoring many festivals held in Hongdae. . . . Moreover, we put our efforts on planning many other cultural programs and supporting young musicians at home and abroad. We aim to be the best communicator in this local area helping them harmonize. Club Culture Association combines various club contents into one for young generation and local society in Hongdae so that here could become a culture liberated area for whom loves music and dance.

Choi, as the CCA representative, explained its objective of cultural intervention and mediation to me.[11] Yet when he first arrived in Hongdae, Choi was more interested in place marketing than in Hongdae culture itself. In 2006, he posted this comment on the Hongdae Culture Academy Internet bulletin board: "At first I saw this area from the perspective of an outsider. That is, I approached this area as a place for foreign visitors during the 2002 World Cup from the prospect of place marketing." Lee, another founding member of the CCA, explained his engagement in the association as political intervention and cultural activism. He described his role that of as a cultural coordinator and planner:

> My role is networking. I'm a coordinator. I have no intention to do business or acquire space or form any organization here. . . . [P]lanners are coordinators. Cultural planners should intervene in politics as cultural activists. They should make a connection with and link people and get involved with local governments. I think it's about the politics of intervention.[12]

The leading members of the CCA saw themselves not as cultural workers or businessmen running clubs but as cultural activists. Indeed, Choi remarked in an interview that those who insisted on returning to an earlier Hongdae culture were trying to make Hongdae "a feudal village where subsistent villagers produce and consume what they need."[13] This idea of returning to an earlier Hongdae culture, according to him, was "idealistic, which was not able to construct an appropriate community in the era of soft-capitalism." He elaborated that he aimed to construct a "digital village where people can produce and consume at the global level, and club culture could be a starting point to build an integrated system to run culture and economy." In a similar vein, Lee also remarked that Hongdae could be a model of an ideal community that could showcase the successful symbiosis of culture and economy.[14]

The leading figures of the CCA depicted the dance clubs as an environment where people concurrently play the roles of both consumers and producers.[15] By simultaneously producing and consuming club culture, Choi claimed, "DJs, club staff members, clubbers, and club visitors played the role of prosumers, or the overlapping role of cultural producer and consumer."[16] He asserted that "prosumers possessed the potential to construct a self-sufficient community that would nurture new social and economic relations to incorporate cultural production into economic production." He stressed that to promote such a new ecology of cultural and economic systems, the dance club business should be legalized.

The term "prosumer" generally refers to the blurring of the roles of consumers and producers in close association with a high degree of customization led by the participation of consumers in product-design processes. Choi opined that music production in the era of technology would enable consumers to participate in the process of music production, and the dance clubs would be the sites of music production as well as music markets.[17] The dance clubs were seen as a medium linking culture and economy; people turned their artistic creativity into creative products. By coperforming and cocreating club culture, people transformed a cultural activity into an economic one. Overall, the CCA actively produced discourses about club culture and prosumers. It highlighted that the dance clubs facilitated the ecology of the endogenous cultural and economic movements that shifted the existing boundaries of the cultural and the economic.

The discourses about club culture and prosumers were the very issues that made people outside the dance club sector criticize the CCA for being hegemonic and manipulative. In particular, the self-assertion that the dance clubs together with prosumers were making a new economic system to run Hongdae offended those who regarded Hongdae as a place for artistic ingenuity and creativity. Some people also harbored antagonism toward the discourse of club culture. There was speculation that the CCA coined the term on the pretext of becoming the main stakeholder in the Hongdae project:

> Recently, people easily associate club culture with the clubs or Club Day. . . . I think this kind of association is dangerous since there are many musicians in other clubs as well. They are highly ranked in Korean pop music, and they lead independent culture. But the public does not pay attention to them and instead roughly categorizes everything as club culture. They [the dance clubs] argue that club culture is an attraction for tourism and cultural events. I find it a very superficial approach.[18]

Some people cast skepticism toward Choi because they saw him as an outsider. He was regarded as new compared to the majority of the people from the non-dance-club sectors who had studied, worked, or lived in Hongdae since the 1980s or even the 1990s. In contrast, Choi came to Hongdae in 2000 to participate in the preparations for the 2002 World Cup. He was once a laborer-cum-activist, organizing a labor union in a factory when he was an undergraduate during the 1980s. Because of his involvement in the labor union, Choi was expelled from the university. Subsequently, he worked in Seoul's subway labor union and pioneered the environmental movement and community-making movement in the 1990s. Notably, he united small shops in Insadong to protest against the dominance of franchise stores. This movement was crucial in pushing the authorities to initiate the CD policy in Insasdong. Because of Choi's previous career paths, people from the non-dance-club sectors regarded the CCA as his political platform. One member of the HCAC told me, "I don't know what he really wants here. I don't know whether he knows culture. . . . I guess that he's a typical activist who sets agendas and dominates people and resources."[19] Cho, a lead figure of the non-dance-club sectors who initiated the organization of their own group, also shared his opinion of Choi with me: "He [Choi] finally saw that culture is something interesting for him to intervene in. Now Hongdae has been infiltrated by a group of political activists."[20]

Becoming Hongdae Natives

In January 2004, twenty people gathered to establish the HCAC. The group included a performing artist, a live club manager, a film/documentary maker, an architect, a reporter, six gallery curators, and seven people engaged in cultural event planning companies and NGOs.[21] One of the participants, a cultural program planner, was previously engaged in writing the Hongdae place-marketing report. Thus members from both the CCA and the HCAC had participated in authoring the report, and most likely members of both organizations were informed about the report's content.

The participants started the inaugural meeting by introducing themselves. Many spoke about how long they had worked and lived in Hongdae (in general, between fifteen and thirty-five years). They expressed concerns about the status quo, which included the financial difficulties encountered by Theatre Zero; soaring rental rates; poor working conditions; changing local situations, such as the influx of new businesses and people; and the HCD project. In particular, Theatre Zero became a topic for heated discussion as rent hikes pressured the performance theater to cease operations. The theater manager was a significant figure in Hongdae. He was a founding member of the legendary café Gompangee in the early 1990s, which was widely regarded as the birthplace of Hongdae culture. Gompangee was a multifunctional place that served as a café, performance theater, dance hall, and gallery. Theatre Zero's financial problems thus generated bitter feelings among the local artists. The participants shared their concern that the CD project would escalate rent hikes.

Twelve participants—seven of whom were engaged in event planning and NGOs—attended the second HCAC meeting.[22] The participants decided to utilize the opening of the HCAC as a public forum to discuss Theatre Zero's predicament, the rent crisis, and the CD project. They elected Cho to lead the HCAC. Cho had lived in Hongdae since 1985 when he was a student at Hongik University. He was the bass guitarist of Whyangshinhye Band, one of the first generation of Hongdae independent music bands. Cho published a local magazine and organized a flea market called Hope Market. He once ran for office as a local representative but was not elected. When he became the HCAC representative, he was operating a cultural event agency while working part time at a restaurant and a laundry shop.

The HCAC staged a campaign for Theatre Zero at its opening ceremony, along with a performance about the death of artists and an open forum to discuss the CD project. HCAC membership, according to the flyer distributed during the ceremony, amounted to approximately 120 individuals and 30 organizations.[23] The HCAC publicized its mission statement, demanded a resolution to the rental hikes, and called for the participation of cultural workers and artists in the policy project:

> The Hongdae Culture and Arts Cooperation (tentative) is a group of local artists and cultural workers . . . established as a voluntary local cultural association in order to solve the agendas of the local cultural issues. . . . Prepare practical support for the infrastructure and corporations for Hongdae culture and arts so that we can cope with the soaring rent! Ensure institutional participation of the local artists and cultural workers in the cultural district project![24]

The opening ceremony received much press coverage and resonated deeply with artists and cultural workers. A TV news program from the Korean Broadcasting System (KBS) reported on the angry voices and gestures some artists displayed toward the policy project:

> The independent space of Hongdae area, the core of underground culture and nonmainstream culture, is facing extinction. Rent has been rocketing since the Seoul city government decided to make it a cultural district. Many artists have to move out because of high rent.[25]

Such emotional responses stemmed partly from the reputation and association of Hongdae with resistant culture and partly from the mobilization of networks by some HCAC members who were engaged in cultural activism, the Korean art scene, and the popular music scene. In particular, the HCAC collaborated with Cultural Action to draw media attention to Theatre Zero's predicament. The first cultural NGO in Korea, Cultural Action was established in 1999 by scholars and cultural critics to achieve cultural democracy.[26] As a firm supporter of independent culture, this NGO empowered the voice of the HCAC through strategic mobilization of public opinion.

The media presented Theatre Zero's predicament by framing local artists and cultural workers as victims of commercialization processes and claiming that the CD project would only aggravate their situations. Responding to the media coverage, the district government mediated between the theater owner and the owner of the building to negotiate the rental prices and also formed a committee for the project. The fifteen-member committee comprised district council members, experts engaged in cultural administration, local artists, local businessmen, and residents. Notably, four members within the committee constituted the artist group, three of whom were from the HCAC.

The HCAC began to claim that "real Hongdae culture" should be promoted and that "real Hongdae people" should take part in the making of the CD project. The expression "Hongdae people" was commonly used to refer to artists, residents, students, and businesspeople in Hongdae. Generally, the shared feeling toward working and living in Hongdae made people regard themselves as belonging to the community of Hongdae people. However, labeling some Hongdae people as "real" conveyed disapproval of certain others. It carried a sense of historicity and ownership of Hongdae, and such sentiments were emphasized during the HCAC meetings. An organizer of a cultural event company told me, "We need to have an exhibition about the subjects of Hongdae culture. I have collected all the articles about it since the 1990s. I can bring them here. We have to bring all the materials and documents showing the real history of this place."[27] HCAC meeting minutes from January 2004 note, "Now we have to display who are the subjects of Hongdae culture and what we have been doing."[28]

Interestingly, "Hongdae natives" began to emerge as a new term. Cho started using the expression "Hongdae natives" when the HCAC was established: "Cho, the representative of the Hongdae Culture and Arts Cooperation . . . said that he is a self-appointed Hongdae native. He calls all the artists who have settled in Hongdae, the Hongdae native."[29] The term "Hongdae natives" implies Hongdae is a village populated by indigenous people. As the term was advanced by the HCAC representative, the organization came to be perceived as a group of, or for, the indigenous inhabitants of Hongdae. "Natives" further implies the existence of nonnatives, or "newcomers" and "outsiders." Cho remarked to me that "recently unqualified outsiders polluted Hongdae culture and only local artists were able to maintain its quality."[30] The term "Hongdae natives" thus served to naturalize the HCAC's legitimacy over the representation of Hongdae and the political leverage of the policy project. A member of the CCA commented, "Read carefully what Hongdae Culture and Arts Cooperation means. They [the key members] define what constitutes Hongdae culture. They wield their symbolic power to decide what should constitute culture."[31]

In fact, Cho admitted that "real artists" would not appear at the organization because they regarded it as a "political gathering."[32] He expressed that he did not like politics, but he had to organize the group and become a stakeholder of the policy project in order not to lose Hongdae:

In fact, many people were against the cultural district . . . now those who have interests in it are property owners and those who are bustling about Hongdae culture, including me. . . . We want to hang around and produce something together. Even if we have to borrow institutional forces, we want to keep this community as long as we can save some spaces for us.[33]

Another HCAC member also opined that the establishment of the HCAC was inevitable because other people formed their own organizations: "I tell you again that Hongdae is a place where we don't need any organization. . . . In general, people here don't care what others are doing . . . but others made a group and systematically organized people and resources."[34]

Although the HCAC was established based on the shared sentiment of being Hongdae people, it was in no way a uniform group. Its members held diverse occupations in the fields of music, art, design, media, festival organization, and film. Individual artists and cultural workers rarely participated in its meetings. Attendance was very low, considering the number of registered members. Most of the participants were event and program planners. To a certain extent, their social influences and networks contributed to the HCAC's establishment. However, their dominance in the organization raised questions of whether they had in effect mobilized local dissent for the pursuit of their own interests. One member was rather pessimistic about the future of the HCAC because he anticipated that there would always be a clash of interests due to the diversity of its members.[35]

Despite the heterogeneity of the HCAC's membership, its representative emphasized that Hongdae people should write their own stories by themselves rather than leave the task to "intellectuals" who flocked to and left Hongdae: "Intellectuals once came Hongdae. But they found out that Hongdae is too small for them. . . . Now when I submit applications for grants and funds, they are sitting as executive members of the board reviewing my application forms."[36] The term "Hongdae natives" thus serves partially to demonstrate HCAC members' determination to narrate Hongdae culture by themselves.

The Culture War

For almost an entire year during the policy feasibility review process, HCAC and CCA members met at public forums and hearings.[37] On such occasions, the confrontation between the two organizations concerning whether dance clubs were part of Hongdae culture intensified. Furthermore, defining Hongdae culture as an explicit cultural genre emerged as problematic. HCAC members were especially concerned because Hongdae culture had long been associated with particular attitudes rather than genres. Thus, they focused on describing the value of Hongdae culture, not defining it. One post on the HCAC Internet bulletin board in 2004 said, "The value of Hongdae culture is a set of virtues, such as being independent, alternative, creative, and experimental."

This set of virtues—alternative, creative, and experimental—served as the normative standard and drew the line between what belonged to Hongdae culture and what did not. HCAC members depicted themselves as guardians of creative Hongdae culture while describing the dance clubs as the main actor responsible for the commercialization of Hongdae culture. The same 2004 Internet bulletin board post said, "I think the present dance clubs are rather close to alcohol and dance houses. They are not cultural places. My opinion is that all the clubs not involved in creative performances should disappear." Some HCAC members said that the term "club culture" reflected the CCA representative's political ideologies. Club culture, according to them, was neither creative nor authentic. Rather, it was contrived and political. Therefore, dance clubs were not qualified to stand among Hongdae culture.

Meanwhile, the CCA representative criticized such a qualification-oriented distinction between Hongdae culture and non-Hongdae culture for being "exclusive," "elitist," and "individualistic."[38] Choi even described Hongdae as "an epitome of artists detached from the local society and decadent culture of musicians."[39] He remarked that, as such, the present Hongdae culture should become more communicative and open to the masses.[40] He also said that Hongdae culture in the 1990s went through a "primitive phase" and in the 2000s entered a "structural phase."[41] He argued that the current Hongdae culture should be updated to fit the changing social and cultural circumstances, or it would lose its prospects for self-renewal. His understanding of Hongdae culture was based on the perspective of progressivism, which views culture as a process that develops from a primitive stage toward a complex system:

> The existence of artists is not trivial. Yet Hongdae in the 1990s should be changed to keep up with the times. This original form could not keep up with the new period. Structures for cultural consumption and production are changing. Hongdae in the 1990s was in a primitive stage, in which the identity and basis of Hongdae culture were forming, that is, a kind of stage for occurrence. But when it entered the 2000s, a new structure was needed for delivering Hongdae culture to the masses. The old Hongdae culture of the 1990s, I think, was not successful in that matter.[42]

Furthermore, Choi highlighted that those who developed the alternative and resistant Hongdae culture in the 1990s came to possess vested interests in monopolizing Hongdae culture in the 2000s. Musicians and artists led the cultural movements in the 1990s by challenging the elitist point of view on performance proper. This was why he criticized the HCAC for having fossilized Hongdae culture.

The CCA and the HCAC, based on their normative ideas about Hongdae culture, envisioned how the future HCD should look. The CCA's vision was explicit and simple: the HCD should promote nonconventional and emerging cultural activities. Therefore, it strongly argued that the future cultural district should acknowledge dance clubs as cultural places and thus legalize the dance club business:

> Club culture has newly reconstructed the local culture to cope with the changing realities of the locality. This club culture is a very new form of culture, which can serve to develop Seoul as a cultural city. Therefore, the Space Culture Centre, the Hongdae Shinchon Culture Forum, and 157 people from 11 organizations and 3,238 citizens in-

cluding foreigners petitioned to make the Hongdae club culture district. . . . Since the core of Hongdae culture is cultural diversity, the focus of the future cultural district should lie in providing programs for underground, independent, and nonmainstream cultural activities including people, organizations, and facilities related to them.[43]

In contrast, the HCAC was unable to come up with a uniform vision about the HCD. HCAC members were aware of it as a public project and therefore discussed what would justify the spending of public resources in Hongdae. The following comment was posted on the HCAC Internet bulletin board in 2004:

> Honestly, we are doing business, namely cultural business. What I'm doing is also for making money. . . . [B]ut is it right and of conscience that we claim the bloodlike tax money taken from other people, who have to work from dawn to night, and which I hate, to be used for supporting our businesses?

This discussion process led HCAC members to search for common goals with the authorities. They proposed some possible projects such as the renovation of environments; the creation of parks, galleries, and performance stages; and the development of cultural education programs. They said that such projects could give them more room for negotiation with the authorities.

HCAC members generally agreed that the future cultural district should promote Hongdae as a center for independent culture. As more meetings took place, however, different ideas about how to operate the district emerged. For example, the representative of one cultural festival argued that those people who could manage multicultural spaces could contribute to uniting various cultural genres and revitalizing the diversity of Hongdae culture. By emphasizing the "original diversity," he implied that Hongdae culture should not be oriented toward any specific sector. In 2004 he posted, "I see that our task is to recover the original diversity of the local culture. Isn't that the reason why we are together here? Although we are from different professions and backgrounds, aren't we in the process of coordinating a new vision for Hongdae?" Overall, actors in event planning and networking emphasized that all people from various genres should unite and create a common vision.

However, some HCAC members who had been working in the art and design sector envisioned the future cultural district as a space for art. These people mostly graduated from Hongik Art College and shared the feeling that they had created Hongdae as an art place. Ahn, a professor from the college, highlighted the importance of art for constructing Hongdae. Although Ahn was not an HCAC member, he was widely regarded as the godfather of Hongdae people. According to Cho, Hongdae culture was the outcome of the imagination of Ahn.[44] The professor was a pioneer in electronic art, and he opened Electronic Café, the first multicultural café in Hongdae, in the 1980s. Long before Hongdae became widely known to the public, he proposed the creation of a "Hong party" to unite artists based in Hongdae. In 2004 Ahn commented during a seminar, which was quoted on the HCAC Internet bulletin board, that the HCD should be a center for Korean modern art:

> I became a student [of Hongik Art College] in 1970 and have been here for thirty-three years. I think if Hongdae disappears, then the Korean culture and art scene would vanish too. . . . I think the art college made it possible that the music and performing arts scenes were able to originate from here. Therefore, the cultural district should support mainly the art sector by making the locale as a basement of the Korean modern art for the globalization of the Korean art.

Ahn prioritized the art sector among others as the driving force to lead the rest of the cultural scenes.

Freelance workers and artists, however, expressed their wish for the policy project to address the issues of minimum living standards and subsidies to support cultural production rather than the construction of centers and organizations. In fact, Cho wanted to utilize the project to gain funds and subsidies. He was against constructing any cultural center because he thought such a place would benefit only a few organizations and consequently become an exclusive league. Rather, Cho suggested that the CD project should support cultural production financially:

> How many people can be accommodated there [at the cultural center]? Twenty people per year? I heard that Seoul Cultural Foundation started supporting organizations or groups that have more than five members. The sponsorship, I heard, was more than 15,000,000 won per year. This amount of money sounds quite generous. The policy could do that.[45]

There even emerged a voice that proposed nullifying the policy project on the basis of the limitations of policy intervention in promoting spontaneous cultural activities. Kim, the representative of the Live Club Union and who had worked for the legalization of the live club business in the 1990s, asked during a seminar whether the project was indeed necessary for the locale. He was quoted on the HCAC Internet bulletin board in 2004:

> I want to raise the issue of whether we need any governmental support. Previously, we argued that Hongdae culture is facing a crisis and therefore we need to take advantage of the cultural district. I think we should think about how to activate Hongdae culture. Maybe we don't need to consider the policy at all. I suggest that we should reflect upon ourselves to deal with the crisis of Hongdae culture.

During my interview with Kim, he expressed concerns that HCAC members were inexperienced in terms of working with the authorities, and they did not prepare concrete schemes and strategies to fully utilize the policy project.[46] One HCAC member highlighted that the project would provoke fights over governmental resources among HCAC members:

> I wanted to attend the last meeting but I didn't. Because I felt I would have fought with others if I had been there. He [one of the HCAC members] argued that he needed an alternative space. Okay, it is fine to bring in that story. Then who operates it, if there is such a space? That is his calculation. He said that he would. But it is out of the question. Regardless of who occupies the space, it will be a problem.[47]

As this comment highlights, the policy preparation process revealed differences among HCAC members regarding what constitutes Hongdae culture and also conflicting opinions over the distribution of resources under the policy project.

The competing visions of the project reflected the diverse interests of the local actors. The actors, however, avoided expressing their economic and political interests directly. Instead, they conveyed their interests via cultural discourses like the "promotion of creativity," "new forms of culture," "creative spaces," "the center of Korean modern art," and "the original diversity of Hongdae culture."[48] However, both the CCA and the HCAC came to emphasize the normative values that would allow something to qualify as Hongdae culture. HCAC members highlighted that

Hongdae culture should have creativity and originality. By asserting these characteristics, they interpreted artistic creativity as noncommerciality and originality as the exclusive patent through which to secure exclusive ownership of Hongdae culture. The CCA, meanwhile, claimed that Hongdae culture should be progressive and open, thereby expanding cultural activities to include social evolution.

A Journey to Becoming Something New

As Chapter 2 explores, the CD policy treats culture as authenticity, as an exclusive substance to be protected from market reasoning as well as a uniqueness that creates added value and hence increases market competence. The Hongdae place-marketing report—by reframing a locality and its residents as the objects, targets, means, and subjects of marketing—equates being in a city with being in the market. At the same time, by interpreting cultural politics as a part of place-marketing schemes, the report turns cultural activism into the effort to transcend market rules by enhancing cultural authenticity and place identity to achieve market competence. Therefore, people's capacity to possess imagination and the hands-on capability to synthesize personal traits and skills and to produce added value—in order to create authentic culture (cultural products) and places (vibrant urban milieus)—becomes problematized. The basic message of the Hongdae place-marketing report is that one should become self-organized to play multiple roles and secure tenancy in a market-cum-city to avoid being displaced from Hongdae. Under this framework, Hongdae cultural workers and artists are saddled with the pressure to verify cultural autonomy by achieving financial self-sufficiency. "Place imagineer" and "cultural engineer" disseminate a self-image very similar to the enterprising self—or the self-supporting person responsible for cultural, political, and economic self-reliance.

Both the CCA and HCAC strategically selected and mobilized policy ideas that comprised ambiguous notions of cultural politics, place marketing, and active citizenship. By interpreting culture as capital to be transferred to social relations and economies, the CCA presented the dance clubs as sites that witnessed the emergence of a new cultural and economic agency: the prosumer.

The HCAC appealed to the notion of culture as an exclusive substance of a unique entity and cultural politics as cultural protectionism and anti-commercialism. It therefore emphasized historicity and authenticity as the criteria to claim cultural and spatial ownership of Hongdae. These notions made the HCAC depict a confrontational situation with natives versus outsiders, the cultural versus the commercial, and artistic creativity versus political tactics.

Chapter 2 examines how subculture was invoked to link the multifaceted projects of becoming autonomous citizens, subverting elitist institutions, and restructuring the national economy. It also investigates how the intersection of these goals initiated the Hongdae project in pursuit of symbiosis between culture and economy, which resulted in the dissemination of the entrepreneurial subjectivity. Based on such explication of the inscription of the cultural turn in the Hongdae project, this chapter explores how the entrepreneurial subjectivity has been experienced in locally specific contexts. Giving attention to the embodiment of social forces in a particular locality is to explore path dependence and social exchange in understanding social change. Subjectification is both a disciplinary practice and a self-reflexive practice. Becoming natives and prosumers demonstrates one path to entrepreneurialism embodied in the post-financial-crisis transformation in Seoul.

Overall, Hongdae natives and prosumers both sought liberation: the natives pursued liberation from depersonalization and the commodification of human beings, while the prosumers sought liberation from the segmentation of cross-societal relations. At stake, however, is whether natives and prosumers are the imposed subjectivities as a major requisite to play the policy game. It seems that the Hongdae project, even before it was enforced, triggered a socialization process through which new subjectivities of citizens were disseminated, encountered, and internalized.

4

Becoming Intermediaries

The feasibility review and administrative plan for the HCD project were released in December 2004. According to the feasibility study, Hongdae seemed perfect to be the future district of a multicultural space. However, in 2005 the city and district governments decided to postpone the project indefinitely. What led the authorities to cancel the project? What was the impact of the policy cancelation on Hongdae? This chapter examines the policy cancelation as an outcome of contradictory policy ideas. It argues that the unexecuted project offered a new occasion through which people contemplated a new challenge: how a good culture can make a good business.

Hongdae came to be filled with high-rise buildings, cafés, shops, restaurants, and international tourists. In 2006 the Seoul Cultural Foundation, an umbrella organization of the city government, sponsored a new forum called the Hongdae Culture Academy as a gesture to construct a post-CD Hongdae. Key members from the CCA and the HCAC joined the forum. Surprisingly, the parties who used to condemn the commercialization of Hongdae culture now wanted a part in its market success. Some participants proposed a new role, that of intermediary, to create a system to generate money.

Policy as planned intervention does not always entail planned outcomes. The announcement of the policy project in 2003 to some extent gave birth to the CCA and the HCAC. The policy preparation process revealed the vested interests attached to Hongdae culture and led to the (re)configuration of local relations. Policy cancelation became a new condition for social changes in post-CD Hongdae, where participants of the newly formed academy proposed a new self-description. This chapter elucidates the performative capacity of the policy ideas, suggesting that although the Hongdae project itself was never executed, the policy ideas made an impact on the reconfiguration of citizen subjectivities and social relations.

A Multicultural Space

A research center affiliated with Hongik University had conducted the policy feasibility review. Some people expressed concern that any outcome of the review might unduly favor those associated with the art college. The report focuses on these concerns and notes that local people had been sensitive toward the review process.[1] It states that the outcome was crucial to determine the future of Hongdae and highlights many events that took place during the review process. These include Theatre Zero's rent predicament, the real estate boom, the mushrooming of dance clubs, and the establishment of the HCAC and the CCA.[2] The report further notes that the conventional standards used to distinguish the cultural from the commercial could not be harnessed to evaluate Hongdae culture effectively. It thus proposes that Hongdae should be approached as a "multicultural" space and as a new model of "a community" combining "play, culture, economy, and community."[3]

According to the feasibility review, Hongdae comprises "an art space, a quality café space, an underground club culture space, and a cultural business working space, which makes a multicultural space."[4] Cafés, clubs, and culture-related business establishments are included as multicultural spaces because they are seen as possessing "quality." The image created by such diverse multicultural spaces is deemed essential to make Hongdae a fitting locale to market the city:

> The key words which represent the identity of Hongdae are non-mainstream "art" and "music" based on creativity and experimentalism. . . . The area is a multicultural space, which consists of various cultural characteristics. The art space, quality café space, underground club culture space, and cultural business working space constitute this multicultural space. . . . Because of these place images, now the area distinguishes itself as a suitable place for city marketing. Furthermore, the development of neighboring places will even increase the value of the area.[5]

Based on the conceptualization of Hongdae as a multicultural space, the review recommends reshaping Hongdae as a district for "alternative culture and arts."[6] The term "alternative" is somewhat ambiguously addressed in various dimensions throughout the review assessment. It is associated with a cultural genre ("alternative culture"), a method of doing art ("alternative production of art beyond traditional means"), and a type of exhibition venue ("alternative space"). In short, "alternative" connotes a genre, a method, and a place. To promote alternative culture and arts under the policy project, the report recommends certain venues be designated cultural facilities. These venues include exhibition halls, small-scale theaters, clubs, publishers, studios, bookshops, art academies, art shops and framing stores, record shops, craft shops, ceramic shops, and educational facilities.[7] Such diversity demonstrates that the term "alternative" is a justification for appointing certain shops and business establishments as multicultural venues.

What, then, distinguishes the usual shops and business establishments from the alternative ones? What distinguishes an ordinary café from a quality café? The feasibility review explains that "artistic minds" could transform ordinary business establishments into multicultural places. An existing restaurant is cited as an example. The owner, who possessed an "artistic mind," had utilized the restaurant space to exhibit modern Korean and Western gramophones and to host a music hall and gallery.[8] This example shows that if people motivated by their artistic minds could perform cultural activities in a shop and/or a business, such an establishment could then become a multicultural place. The meaning of "multicultural" in this context is thus closer to the multifunctionality of a place.

Such space-oriented interpretation of "multicultural" can be seen partly as a strategic gesture that embodies the claims of local actors who present their workplaces as cultural places. The feasibility review describes "shops and studios" as the "catalyst places of alternative and independent culture":

Many art shops and studios around Hongik University were the major sites of Hongdae in the 1980s. It was Hongdae people based in Hongik Art College who formed these sites. Their sentiment and creativity were the catalyst for the birth of alternative and independent culture.[9]

This excerpt is almost identical to the self-description of the HCAC. Likewise, the following description of the dance clubs in the review is similar to the self-presentation of the CCA:

In general, clubs are multicultural spaces where unique music, dance, people, and communication coexist. In other words, advanced and diverse music genres in the clubs (advanced rock, techno, etc.), which are leading the latest trends, enable people to be open-minded, soothe worn-out bodies and souls, and to provide them hope for life.[10]

The following excerpts indicate how the dance clubs saw themselves:

Club culture space is healthy leisure space where people dance and appreciate the cutting edge music that DJs and artists create. . . . Club space, which emerged endogenously in Hongdae, is now used as cultural space where many foreigners and cultural workers engaged in a diverse range of domains communicate with each other via body language, dancing, and thereby make cultural communities.[11]

We [the CCA] aim to be the best communicator in this local area helping them [young musicians] harmonize. We combine various club contents into one for the young generation and local society in Hongdae so that here could become a culture-liberated area for those who love music and dance.[12]

"Club" is defined as *a multicultural space with unique music, dance, people, and communication.* And "club cultures" are defined as the unique youth subculture, which are generated, shared, and change around the club space. Club cultures are characterized as "taste culture, party culture," "alternative culture, digital culture," and "local culture, community culture."[13]

These excerpts illustrate how the CCA advocated for the clubs as multicultural spaces where music, dance, and communication coevolved. The same content appears in the feasibility review.

Although the feasibility review recommends the appointment of certain shops, clubs, and business establishments as cultural facilities, the question of whether these can be legally acknowledged as such became a thorny issue. The review concedes that the existing legal definition of "culture" was too narrow to encapsulate Hongdae culture. It therefore proposes that the relevant authorities revise the legal definition. At that time, the Ministry of Health and Welfare and the Ministry of Culture and

Tourism oversaw legislation concerning public hygiene and cultural administration. Hongdae's establishment as a multicultural space depended, in fact, on these ministries' legal oversight and concerted administration. This issue of revising the legal code resulted in the indefinite postponement of the policy project. Although the relevant officials from the city and district governments acknowledged the cultural significance of club culture and independent culture, they commented that the need for the legalization of the dance club business made the authorities cautious about the policy's implementation.[14]

Lee from the CCA commented that any policy implementation without the legalization of the dance club businesses would not achieve its objective of fostering a multicultural space.[15] Choi, the CCA representative, said that although he had advocated for the policy project initially, he subsequently came to think that the project's postponement would be better for the locale if the ambiguities surrounding the legal status of the dance club business remained unresolved.[16] Cho from the HCAC recalled that the majority of its members were doubtful about the policy project and questioned whether the policy itself was in fact suitable for Hongdae.[17] Overall, the policy postponement was a tacit negotiation between the local actors, on the one hand, who had realized hasty project enforcement would not benefit the locale, and the authorities, on the other hand, who were keen to avoid complicated administrative procedures.

Becoming Cultural Intermediaries

Various changes in Hongdae emerged in the aftermath of the policy cancelation. For one, Cho stepped down as the representative of the HCAC and left Hongdae, where he had lived since the 1980s.[18] He became a farmer instead. According to Choi, the internal solidarity among the dance clubs weakened considerably since the mid-2000s.[19] Some clubs wanted to withdraw from the CCA to expand their businesses in other areas of Seoul.

Efforts to promote post-CD Hongdae also emerged. In January 2006, the Seoul Cultural Foundation sponsored the launch of the Hongdae Culture Academy to foster private and public partnership among the area inhabitants. The academy aimed to forge a local forum to discuss the future of Hongdae. Kim, the new HCAC representative, took the lead in organizing the academy's events. At that time, Kim was the owner of a live club as well as a representative of both the Live Club Union and the weekly art market called Free Market. The academy offered lectures, workshops, and courses on business management, marketing skills, and public relations strategies. Hongdae Culture Academy participants were engaged in various organizations including the HCAC, the CCA, governmental institutions, universities, industries, and NGOs. Many of them also participated in planning cultural events and festivals.

The launch of the academy highlighted several important changes in the locale. First, the CCA and the HCAC started communicating with each other; their participation in the academy can be seen as a gesture of reconciliation. The CCA representative was invited to share his ideas on how to construct a new cultural and economic system in Hongdae. He asserted that independent and underground culture should be redefined to keep pace with an information society:

> In the age of the information society, we should reinterpret independent and underground culture. . . . Maybe this kind of approach is different from the position of the first Hongdae generation, particularly regarding how to connect culture and market and how to construct a cultural infrastructure. . . . We ought to think about what we should create in new situations and conditions.[20]

In other words, Choi acknowledged the earlier criticism from the HCAC—that the dance clubs underestimated artistry and creativity—and replied that the dance clubs were exploring appropriate measures to foster these qualities.

Kim responded that the live clubs should learn from the CCA's systematic management to help independent musicians overcome stagnation. He elaborated that the club management should help musicians, who were like "manual laborers," perform their work more professionally:

> Generally, musicians in the live clubs work like they are manual laborers. But the Sound Day [an event organized by the CCA] team even has its planning chair, which works very professionally. I think we should learn from it. . . . We are now attempting a new media business. . . . Contrary to the previous one like a manual guide book, I imagine it would be a link to connect media and content. . . . I feel that we are stuck. We need a new breakthrough but can't come up with a new idea.[21]

The new HCAC representative said that his engagement with the policy project had stimulated self-reflection, which in turn prompted him to see the "narrow-mindedness" of Hongdae people:

> There was a lack of experience and recognition on how to let the inner energy of Hongdae people communicate with people from the outside, and how to construct new relationships with them. Hongdae people would always say, "It's not Hongdae style." It could be a free and idiosyncratic way of thinking, but seen from another aspect, it is narrow-mindedness. I think the experience from the Theatre Zero incident and the cultural district project has awakened us. We have come to realize that we can acknowledge others and live in accord with them.[22]

He also highlighted the necessity for Hongdae people to fit into new circumstances and to communicate with the outside world: "People should change themselves according to the changing circumstances. Now, the problem is that people are left behind, regressing from the social trends."[23] What made Kim compare musicians in the live clubs to manual laborers? Why did he come to associate Hongdae style with narrow-mindedness? Why did he assert that people should change themselves to fit their circumstances? Other seminar participants implicitly answered these questions.

During one discussion, Lee, who was introduced as the director of an art management company and representative of an event planning company, pinpointed that conversations about Hongdae culture used to end with queries about whether Hongdae culture really exists. He said that "physical places, such as cafés, clubs, and galleries, create ambiances, not culture." He continued, "Thus, Hongdae culture does not exist, yet certain values exist."[24] His conclusion—that Hongdae culture does not exist but ambiances embodying certain values do exist—is closely related to the reasons for the policy cancelation. Hongdae culture refers to the quality of things and the concrete substances that embody makers' values. This man asserted that producers should substantiate their values with something concrete, and intermediaries should venture into a distribution system to facilitate the purchase of products by consumers. He emphasized the need to create markets where makers and consumers can meet indirectly; where Hongdae culture in the form of products can be transacted.

Choi, who was introduced as a design critic, also expressed similar concerns over the need to explore various channels through which Hongdae culture can reach a wider audience. Sharing about the changes in his perspective toward Hongdae—from a university area to a district where new cultural trends emerge—he emphasized the need to balance the "arts" and "consumption" to foster Hongdae culture:

> We need to make strategies and objectives about how to effectively extract, visualize, and substantiate arts and culture from Hongdae culture. There is no place in this country that is constituted only by an arts code. How can we achieve a double-code constituted by an arts code and a consumption code? Even though it is hard to achieve, isn't it required to make an art landscape and a consumption landscape coexist?[25]

Many forum participants articulated the existence of markets as a requisite of the reproduction of Hongdae culture. The expressions of self-reflection—such as being narrow-minded, a need to become intermediaries, and a desire to have a balance between arts and consumption—reveal how engagement in the policy project had stimulated people to come to terms with markets. Specifically, they asked how and in what forms the values, quality, and artistic code of Hongdae culture should be objectified and how and where to disseminate such objectified forms to a wider audience. They found their answer in the creation of markets.

Highlighting the reproduction of Hongdae culture, forum participants called for a generational shift to replace the first-generation Hongdae culture. According to Lee, who was introduced as a lead person of a network company, Hongdae culture had acquired the status of "myths" and "fantasies":

> There were some moments when fantasies and myths became important factors to judge Hongdae culture. . . . People engaged in Hongdae culture should deny such fantasies and myths. . . . If people who created Hongdae culture made the memory of Hongdae culture, it cannot be a right answer for now. . . . We are now standing in between the demand from the first Hongdae generation and the demand from the outer world.[26]

The expressions "fantasies" and "myths" imply that Hongdae culture had become insubstantial—almost fictional—and was no longer able to reproduce itself.

Those who addressed the necessity for the evolution of Hongdae culture were mostly engaged in event planning and networking. They were experienced in working with civil organizations and governmental authorities. They had come to Hongdae relatively recently, in the 1990s or the 2000s, compared to the first generation of Hongdae people, who had come to the locale in the 1980s as students, artists, architects, and designers. To break new ground, the newer group emphasized the creation of money-generation systems. They associated market success with the economic independence of Hongdae culture, which would ultimately make Hongdae culture self-sustainable. They thus argued that cultural intermediaries should take the new lead to achieve market success and to create a structure for Hongdae's economic independence:

> We can call cultural intermediaries leading actors who achieve success in markets. . . . Now, Hongdae culture does not have a structure which generates money. Future visions and systematic organizations are absent. . . . We need intermediaries who are ready to act and can make a structure for economic independence.[27]

Intermediaries, not makers, were to determine salable products, devise effective marketing strategies, and explore new markets to propel a new Hongdae culture.

The substance of the forum discussions demonstrates how Hongdae culture came to mean forging new relationships among makers, intermediaries, and consumers. Forum participants asserted the need to revalorize money making and marketing as essential means to reproduce Hongdae culture, not as a sellout of culture:

> In general, culture is, in short, the relationship among producers, intermediaries, and consumers. Hongdae culture tends to seek meanings, but we can't live with meanings. We have to survive. . . . Hongdae people do not have an understanding of the market. They are not producing programs to make money.[28]

Shin, introduced as a music critic, commented, "I suggest that we should sell independent music in the world. Then we have to sing not only in Korean but in other languages. Commercial music is not the same as being sellable in the global market."[29] Paek, introduced as the editor of a design magazine, added, "Marketing decides almost everything. An individual project can be innovative and creative. But how to put such interesting projects together makes a difference."[30]

However, there were also people who disapproved of the new shift toward markets. It should be noted that Cho, the first representative of the HCAC, had refused to talk about Hongdae culture and Hongdae people with me in 2006.[31] While the policy project once prompted Cho to invent the concept of Hongdae natives, the shift toward market in the locale led him to subsequently deny the concept. He anticipated that Hongdae would become one of the numerous, typical commercial areas without any artistic vitality.

After the announcement of the policy project, local cultural workers and artists established collective organizations for the first time. They produced cultural discourses, positioned themselves as legitimate stakeholders, familiarized themselves with laws and administration procedures, and proposed future visions for the locality. As the project evolved, those people engaged in planning and networking—who proved to be more capable in mobilizing discourses and social networks than freelance artists and workers—took the lead in the policy process and local governance. At first, they advocated for protecting Hongdae culture from market forces and disapproved of club culture and its money-making emphasis. Yet these same people eventually came to see money generation as necessary for the reproduction of Hongdae culture.

The participants of the forum as well as a number of interviewees said that the policy experience prompted them to reconsider the balance between arts and consumption, along with their role in reproducing Hongdae culture. The policy cancelation became a new reality for post-CD Hongdae. It offered a new occasion through which people contemplated challenges about what they should become and what they should do.

"Hongdae Has Already Perished"

The Hongdae Culture Academy ended up as a one-off project. Interlocutors who were interviewed after the policy cancelation described the situation more cynically than before. In 2009 one core member of the HCAC said that the policy project was canceled because the policy itself was not suitable for a place like Hongdae. He described the post-CD situation as "mind your own business." Then he added, "Making it through the day in Hongdae is like conducting cultural activism." He said that survival in Hongdae required a sense of duty and responsibility.[32] What he means is that remaining in Hongdae became difficult because rental rates became unaffordable for small-size businesses.

Cho, who left Hongdae after resigning from the HCAC, told me in 2009 that "morality has disappeared in Hongdae." He remarked that "talking about culture is in fact absurd because culture should be all about doing." He elaborated that "real masters just do without talking and would not make any noise." Hongdae culture, according to Cho, came to be produced by "marketing rather than laboring, which is sickening." He asked, "Can we say that we are doing culture without labor?" He doubted whether culture produced without labor would be rooted in "morality." He contrasted "morality" embedded in labor with the "lousiness" of marketing.[33]

Cho's perspective, captured in my interview with him, is abstract and full of metaphors. However, such expressions as "talking about culture is in fact absurd" and "real masters just do without talking," and his beliefs that marketing is "sickening" and "lousy" and that "morality" is embedded in labor disclose his uneasiness about the increasing emphasis on the presentation and management of culture. "Doing culture" and "labor" seem to mean work—that is, making something actual—and prioritize creatorship rather than physical activities per se. In contrast, "talking culture" and "marketing" appear to refer to duplicating and repackaging something rather than creating something new. Sickening and lousy marketing seemingly implies the creation of added value without making something, which is immoral according to Cho.

In 2009 Choi opined that the policy cancelation stemmed from internal dissent among the local actors and the corresponding authorities' lack of understanding about Hongdae culture. In particular, he commented that the crackdown on the dance clubs clearly demonstrated the authorities' ignorance regarding club culture. This incident also made him lose his optimism for successful governance and public-private partnership. As a former prominent civil activist, Choi shared that he still believed in intervention and governance. However, the policy experience made him view "laissez-faire" rather than intervention to be a more effective method in promoting culture. His keywords, he continued, changed from "governance" to "business, market, and individual desire." He explained that governance might have been another name for "enlightenment"; "public interest" might have been a tool to propagate particular ideas.[34]

Choi further elaborated that "individual desire, rather than governance, intervention, and public interest," appeared to be driving culture. He also questioned what could better explain the diversified and enriched cultural content of Hongdae than commercialization. Choi asserted that Hongdae culture should be further commercialized because markets and individual desire, rather than intervention, fostered the Hongdae scene.[35]

Significantly, his emphasis on individual desire and markets as the driving force of culture contradicts his previous campaign for transforming individualistic Hongdae culture to public culture. My 2009 interview elucidates how Choi came to distance himself from activism and public-private partnership as a means to foster Hongdae culture—and turned instead to markets.

Choi had helped Club Day become a great success. It was elevated to a worldwide brand shortly after the 2002 World Cup and became a profitable entrepreneurial venture. Choi thus became widely known as an innovative cultural programmer and marketer. However, Club Day ceased operations in January 2011. Choi explained in an article that the expansion of a number of large, capital-rich dance clubs, such as those owned and operated by YG Entertainment, came to dominate Club Day's content since the mid-2000s.[36]

In a recent interview in 2016, Choi singled out music digitization as a game changer in the mid-2000s.[37] Digitization, he believed, ended the use of clubs as transaction places where cultural production and consumption happened concurrently. Choi elaborated that the production of music had moved to large entertainment houses, and transactions between production and consumption were conducted digitally. Choi admitted that he had failed as the so-called chief executive officer (CEO) of Club Day to upgrade the clubs as transaction places in the digital era. The cessation of Club Day highlighted the onset of digitized, flexible, and monopolized cultural transactions where large-scale entertainment companies produce, market, and circulate digital cultural content. These companies utilize clubs as the venues for publicity and advertising. Indeed, cultural transaction has begun to take place digitally and globally via e-commerce.

Hongdae has undergone rapid changes since the mid-2000s. To a certain extent, the policy cancelation resulted in a situation where governmental intervention in regulating businesses and land usage became unavailable, regardless of whether it would have been effective for Hongdae. Some people have even said that "Hongdae has already perished."[38] New, tall buildings have replaced low-rise residential houses and multiuse buildings. Unused land that had provided artists with space for exhibitions and performances is now filled with shops. The protest against skyrocketing rental rates also continues.

A notable case is the occupation protest in 2009. A restaurant that sold noodles and dumplings was on the verge of forced demolition without proper compensation schemes. The restaurant owner could not recover the deposit she had previously paid to the building owner. To protest both the restaurant's forced eviction and the prevalent practice of paying huge deposits to property owners, independent musicians in Hongdae occupied the restaurant. They strove to inform the public and the authorities about unfavorable lease contract practices toward tenants.

In 2010 the sudden death at age thirty-seven of Moonlight Fairy (Lee Jin Won), an independent musician based in Hongdae, sounded an alarm in the struggle against the monopolistic music and media industry. The musician had been trying to establish a direct transaction route for digitized music between musicians and consumers. In the last ten years, developments in information technology had boosted the expansion of music-streaming markets.[39] This resulted in reductions in the sheer number of offline music outlets and intensified the dominance of online music markets by a handful of big entertainment houses and Internet portal sites. Under the terms set by the oligopolistic music market, Moonlight Fairy was paid in e-money—widely known as *dotori* (acorn)—instead of actual currency for his music from one such portal site. Moonlight Fairy therefore determined to become the distributor of his own digitized music. He also began to openly criticize the unfair profit distribution of digitized music. His premature death, which may have been related to lack of proper care because of struggling finances,[40] stimulated Hongdae musicians to publicize unfair customs in the music industry.

In 2011 another incident united Hongdae musicians to publicize the poor living conditions of people engaged in cultural production. When the owner of Salon Badabie underwent an operation, the bar was nearly forced to shut its doors because of overdue rent. Since its opening in 2004, the bar has provided a place for poetry readings, art exhibitions, and music performances. Some 137 independent music bands voluntarily organized charity concerts for eleven days to collect donations to pay the owner's medical fees and cover the outstanding rent.[41] In summary, the issues of lease, copyright, and digitized music have prompted some people, especially musicians, to contemplate their own survival as makers.

Performative Policy Ideas

Can an unexecuted policy bring about change? That is, can policy *ideas* bring about social change? Chapters 3 and 4 endeavor to answer these questions by demonstrating how the policy ideas embedded in the unexecuted HCD policy project mobilized the reshaping of social relations and the representation of self-descriptions among Hongdae cultural workers and artists.

The pursuit of the three Cs (culture, creativity, and content) pushed the culture industries to the forefront of national economic planning to spearhead postindustrial restructuring toward knowledge-oriented industries. At this nationwide cultural turn, achieving symbiosis between culture and economy thus emerged as an urgent task. The formulation of the Hongdae place-marketing report in 2000 was one of the earliest attempts to transmit the first C (culture) to the second C (creativity) and then to the third C (content). The notion of place marketing exemplified a blueprint that articulated how the transmission from culture to content was imagined. Place marketing also demonstrated a set of paradoxical logics and arguments: it adopted a management framework and applied it to culture (Hongdae culture) and politics (urban governance). It therefore equated cultural and political autonomy with mastering managerial processes and skills.

The shift of the main focus from symbiosis between culture and economy to problematizing the self prompted the Hongdae project to embark on the creation of a new economic agency. This explains why Hongdae Culture Academy programs emphasized the need to establish a new identity and a new role for the survival of Hongdae culture. To varying degrees, the establishment of the CCA, the HCAC, and the Hongdae Culture Academy elucidate "subjectification processes."[42] Members of these organizations observed, redescribed, and remade themselves by articulating what would distinguish them from others: as natives in contrast to nonnatives, as prosumers in contrast to esoteric artists, and as intermediaries in contrast to manual laborers. Hongdae actors thus struggled to find new subjectivities and roles. Meanwhile, they tried to come to terms with a series of local changes that happened within a short span of time. Such changes include the rapidly increasing popularity of the dance clubs; soaring rental rates; and the mushrooming of cafés, tourists, and K-wave products as well as the displacement of some businesses and people.

Scholars have paid attention to gentrification as the main destroyer of Hongdae culture, as "musicians have performed shows and music enthusiasts have bought tickets only to give money to property owners in Hongdae."[43] Club Day, which started as an effort of the dance clubs to adapt to changing socioeconomic conditions, is seen as uprooting Hongdae culture,[44] since the concentration of capital and managerial skills in the dance clubs is perceived to have led to their domination of the Hongdae scene.

The dominance of commercialized dance clubs is seen as the cause of the decline of independent culture, which consequently altered the character of Hongdae and restructured the formation of local businesses.

The preceding explanation attributes the decline of Hongdae to the development and dominance of mass and commercial cultures and their impact on real estate markets and business distribution. These empirical observations are based on a series of events that have taken place since the 2000s: beginning with Club Day in 2001, followed by the Theatre Zero rent issue in 2004, the attempted forceful eviction of the noodle restaurant in 2009, and other cases of displacement related to rental contracts. To a certain extent, dance clubs have contributed to the popularization of Hongdae culture and the increased demand in real estate markets. Yet this does not fully account for the recent gentrification observed in Hongdae.

To increase the availability of land for development, regulations concerning land usage were relaxed in 1994. As a result, between 1994 and 1998, 347.6 square kilometers of semiagricultural land were earmarked for the development of factory sites, residential areas, and restaurant and hotel establishments.[45] Deregulation of land usage was implemented once again immediately after the 1997 financial crisis because the revitalization of the real estate business was regarded as crucial to economic recovery.[46] It was noted that real estate prices plunged 30 percent on average after the financial crisis.[47] A dozen new plans for housing and construction revitalization were enforced between 1998 and 2001. In 1998, for instance, transfer income tax and laws on land transactions were deregulated. At the same time, new schemes to support housing loans and the resale of purchase rights were created. In 1999 plans for the construction of housing and new towns were announced, and the liberalization of housing prices was implemented. In 2001 the housing registration tax was reduced. Seoul and the metropolitan area in particular were directly affected by the various reflationary measures. By 2002, the prices of housing increased some 20 to 30 percent in Seoul and the metropolitan area, compared to their rates two years prior.[48]

Deregulation of real estate markets was accompanied by financial deregulation. In 1993 interest rates regulation was abolished while financial market regulation was relaxed.[49] Financial liberalization was deemed necessary for Korea's transformation from a developmental state to a liberal state. However, financial deregulation without appropriate supervisory measures is seen as the reason for the loss of governmental control over the conglomerates and the financial markets.[50]

In the aftermath of the 1997 financial crisis, the government followed the IMF's programs, which included the pursuit of financial market liberalization and labor market flexibilization. At the same time, the government, with a budget in deficit, chose to revitalize real estate markets via tax reductions, deregulation of real estate transactions, and liquidity support. The combination of deregulation of land usage and the liberalization of financial markets resulted in the influx of speculative capital into real estate markets and strengthened the capitalization of land.[51] The financialization of land, in turn, led to real estate bubbles and inflation.

The observations on the influx of dance clubs, international tourists, and urban amenities in Hongdae can be seen as evidence of the process of "gentrification at the interpersonal level."[52] The confrontational framework—creative versus commercial and resistant culture versus mass culture—might divert attention away from questions on speculative capital and deregulation to turn to the issue of the sellout of subculture. Independent musicians also endeavor to sell their music, and in this sense, indie music is also commercial. Yet selling music does not necessarily mean selling out. In fact, independent music has to be sold to exist.

Ideas shape particular types of socioeconomic projects, and new realities created by such projects affect socioeconomic practices, which in turn affect socioeconomic ideas.[53] The unexecuted CD policy project stimulated people to modify their subjectivities and also led them to ponder a new question: How can good culture make good business? How can value as price be integrated with value as priceless? This new question is explored in Chapter 5.

5

Becoming Laborers, Makers, and Entrepreneurs

The coffee shop used to be considered a "third place"—after home and work—where people create urban public culture.[1] Now it is seen as a place to visualize "gentrification at the interpersonal level."[2] Meanwhile, cheap rent in a city once referred to the use value of land for artists and students, which made it possible for them to forge communities, lead alternative lifestyles, and enjoy mobility provided by public transportation.[3] Today, the cultural cachet created by such artists and students refers to the exchange value of land.

Within the past decade, Hongdae's main scene has shifted from the clubs to the cafés,[4] and the gentrification of the coffee shop has become the talk of the town. Increased rental rates have contributed to the disappearance of cultural workers and artists from Hongdae. Kim Baek Gi, a performing artist who performed at the HCAC opening ceremony in 2004 and has led Korea Performance Art Spirit, a performing art troupe, since 2000, remarks that only some forty to fifty artists have remained in Hongdae, compared to more than a thousand artists who used to stay in the locale. He notes that the first group of artists who left Hongdae comprised those who utilized renovated parking spaces as their studios. The second group included those who needed relatively large venues but could no longer afford the rent. The third group consisted of freelance artists who could not afford to rent even a tiny space.[5] According to a 2016 magazine interview, Kim himself left Hongdae in 2013 and has since settled on Jeju Island.[6] In 2015 a member of the National Assembly produced an audit report on the crisis of Hongdae independent music. The report noted that the twenty-year-old Hongdae scene was about to perish because of rapid commercialization and gentrification.[7] Also, current research on the gentrification of Hongdae documents how Hongdae has become a real estate market.[8]

This chapter focuses on the Hongdae peoples' livelihoods amid gentrification and examines how their firsthand experiences with contemporary urbanism and capitalism have prompted them to reflect on these transformations. It has been observed that those who left or were displaced from Hongdae have resettled in the surrounding neighborhoods by utilizing the established "Hongdae habitus."[9] In other words, these resettlers are exploring new business opportunities and new types of work by leveraging the social networks and cultural capital they previously cultivated in Hongdae. Musicians, artists, translators, merchants, medical doctors, and craftspeople have established cooperatives and also purchased or rented workplaces and residences together.

The HCASC, which was established in 2014, a decade after local musicians and artists had organized the HCAC, is one example of such a co-op. Jung, a band musician and the director of the HCASC, told me that "the HCASC aims to do businesses, because it is a co-op."[10] People from other cooperatives also explain that they pursue "good work and good businesses," doing their "work and career not any economic or social campaign."[11]

Today in Hongdae, some people are beginning to talk about how to make a living rather than how to make culture. Is Hongdae fast becoming a place where people seek alternative economies instead of alternative culture? Why do people still want to stay within or near gentrified Hongdae? The ensuing discussion examines the musicians and cultural workers who attempt to redefine their new socioeconomic roles and seek a new ethic amid neoliberal Hongdae.

Neoliberalism and the Hongdae Style

Cho, the first representative of the HCAC, returned to Hongdae in 2012 after living in the countryside as a farmer. When I interviewed him in 2016, he described himself as a "nomadic laborer" because he was running "several projects simultaneously in varying places."[12] His managing of several short-term contract projects reveals his uncertain livelihood; he is not free and mobile.

Cho raised "economic hardship" and "disenchantment with the community fantasy" as the twin factors that propelled him to leave the countryside. He was unable to earn money and could not get along with the villagers.[13] Cho explained that the tenacious fellowship and neighborliness, which made him feel warmth at the beginning, hampered new trials or ventures in the locale. He was deterred from creating new agricultural products or social events because such trials would eventually shake the already existing social ties and interests interwoven among long-term residents in the small village. Making new relations and products implied an act of treachery to the existing relationships and market rules of the village.

Being away from Hongdae, according to Cho, allowed for a better understanding of Hongdae "from a distance." He described Hongdae as the only place in Korea where people have dreamed for an alternative to capitalism even though Hongdae was located at the center of capitalist development. In this respect, he said, Hongdae is similar to New York as an incarnation of capitalism:

> I did not know about Hongdae because I had always been in it. It [the countryside] was the place where I had stayed farthest away from Seoul. Hongdae is really the only neighborhood in our country where a high school graduate—without a university degree, without money—can bluff in front of a woman. He can go out with a girl [in Hongdae]. In this country [Korea], I came to learn that without a university degree and without money, a man can't marry. It is impossible. Never with a Korean woman. But [in Hongdae], a real cool dude who plays guitar is so popular among girls. . . . Isn't it nice? It [Hongdae] was a village where arts was about to evade the rule of capitalism. . . . Certain territories where capitalism does not operate unite people for collective struggles. As such, it is like a very capitalistic New York. It is dreaming about something different from capitalism while being in the middle of capitalism. Neoliberal capitalist laborers . . . are the spices needed for a city. I hope to have one more place like Hongdae in this country.[14]

According to Cho, a person in Hongdae can be evaluated without having established him- or herself through prerequisites associated with the rules of capitalism such as money and a university degree. What, then, allows a very capitalistic Hongdae to facilitate the negotiation and even evasion of the rules of capitalism? Cho attributes this to the existence of the arts. His description of Hongdae as a territory where arts "evade the rule of capitalism" conveys how the arts function as an alternative value that guides social meanings and behaviors. The arts as an alternative to capitalism in Hongdae can be understood as the critique of standardization and commodification of human beings, as protest against the objectification of actually existing capitalism in Hongdae.

As Cho reiterated, it is ironic that the artistic critique of capitalism and the search for alternativeness thrive most in the very place where capitalism thrives most. Perhaps it is because authenticity is the essential value that underpins the artistic critique of commodification as well as the essential economic value that distinguishes one product from others in markets.

In sharing his experience as a farmer, Cho remarked that "a farmer alone should plan, produce, and explore new markets. A long time ago, everyone was a farmer, a one-person-enterprise." He added, "If a neoliberal world means that a loner/laborer should work hard in one's own ability," it is similar to "the Hongdae style."[15] He explained that in Hongdae, there is the shared idea that individuals are responsible for what they make. Cho thus interprets neoliberalism as the condition in which individuals are given freedom to work and are rewarded according to their work. His understanding of neoliberalism is different from a conventional one—that is, a political doctrine that emphasizes privatization and deregulation and treats market exchange as an ethic to be applied in other realms.[16] In contrast, his interpretation spotlights the attempt of those who regard themselves as artists to link the required work ethic of being self-responsible under neoliberal regimes and the autonomy and individuality required in artistic (cultural) production.

The advancement of the knowledge economy has transformed the notions of the desirable workforce and the working life. Luc Boltanski observes that during the 1990s in particular, capital accumulation processes shifted from mass production to varied and differentiated productions in conjunction with network, financial, and technological development.[17] Accordingly, the desirable features of the firm shifted from being orderly and systematic to being more flexible and less hierarchical. Meanwhile, a new meritocratic approach that values autonomy, creativity, and flexibility emerged as the characteristics of a desirable workforce and of employability.[18] Business corporations came to prioritize the capacity of laborers to synthesize personal traits and skills to create products because the cultural and service industries have become profitable by creating added value from certain qualities of human beings.[19] In other words, labor refers not only to the physical act of working but also to the traits and skills a laborer possesses.

Although Cho emphasizes autonomy and individuality as the essence of cultural production, his comparison of the neoliberal world to the

Hongdae style, to a certain extent, exemplifies the new portfolio of cultural agencies saddled with self-regulation. Cultural workers and artists have emerged as examples of desirable workforces in the post-Fordist era. Indeed, they synthesize their traits, sensibilities, and skills and invest the excess labor in the production of culture anytime and anywhere. This is why their work process is regarded as self-evidently flexible. Tautologically, this flexible work process is claimed to make cultural workers and artists creative, thereby producing new culture.

The capitalization of labor—that is, the transformation of labor into "competence capital"—has been accompanied by a new working rule of "self-control" as a substitute for conventional labor control.[20] A laborer is an enterprise that runs the self. Based on Cho's critical approach to capitalism, it is unlikely that he meant to engage the Hongdae style as a slogan to discipline the self-responsible worker. Rather, Cho appears to understand the precarious livelihoods of cultural workers and artists in the context of neoliberal Hongdae.

Becoming Laborers

The challenges of living in the neoliberal era prompted musicians and artists to organize the HCASC in 2014. Jung, the director of the co-op, explained to me in 2016 that its members aim to create a new business model in Hongdae:

> Seoul's Social Economy District can create a new business model to resolve Hongdae's gentrification. This is one of the projects that the HCASC has been preparing. Other projects are to publicize the local issues and to utilize public spaces and underused spaces for pursuing public interest. Anyway, we are a co-op, so our aim is to do businesses.[21]

In 2011 the city government launched a new program called Social Economy District to create new jobs as well as to solve local sociocultural issues.[22] This program is rooted in concerns regarding the impact of market failures of the capitalist economy, such as inequality, a growing gap between the rich and the poor, and environmental damages. The city government has begun to support social enterprises, neighborhood enterprises, and cooperative associations to alleviate problems created by market failures.

Jung said that the idea to implement the social economy program emerged in 2013, when the mayor met with local artists and cultural workers to discuss Hongdae's gentrification. Jung recalled that the participants highlighted the fact that the freelancers and self-employed members in the former co-op, HCAC, had been inactive, and the operation was largely a nominal one.[23] For this reason, the new co-op has decided to limit membership strictly to individuals and not organizations. In 2016 HCASC's membership stood at fifty-six individuals.

What should cultural workers and artists do to survive, and what about the persistent image of the artist as being detached from everyday life? Jung's thoughts and responses to these questions are worth quoting in full:

> There seems to exist a so-called sense of Korean particularities. We need to be flexible about what it means to be an artist. I don't mean that we should get rid of the pride of being an artist. The image of the artist is, I think, distorted. Artists are seen as those who can live without earning money. Or to the other extreme, they are seen as people who are idle, doing only what they want to do. There is no element of everyday life or an effort to make a living in these two extreme images of an artist. We should get out of this kind of image. In fact, these are what artists have made. I don't see any future if artists are kept in these images. Thus, I think we should be more realistic and understand actuality. There is no artist, I perceive. Yet there is the person doing arts.[24]

During the interview, Jung reiterated that artists should regard themselves as "ordinary people" who work for their livelihoods:

> Artists should perceive themselves as ordinary people making a living. "Because I am a lofty artist, I won't do it." Such a mind-set should be discarded. We should get together at first and then unite with the world. Otherwise, we will be seen as those who live idly. There is still such a perception about artists.[25]

Jung's refusal to be perceived as idle seems to be rooted in the notion of doing art as being in a state of nonwork. This is premised on the association of work with wages and productivity. Within this framework, labor and time spent on artistic production are not considered proper work, and therefore artists' time and labor are overlooked in the calculation of a market price. Jung's refusal to be an artist but rather a "person doing arts" stems from a particular notion of work: one that commands salaries or wages. Here, work is seen as a duty. It entails being serious about one's life and giving up freedom; it requires devoting oneself to the kinds of work that are recognized by others.[26] The association of work with a strong sense of duty explains why freelance cultural workers and artists who do not earn steady salaries or wages are seen as idle or unemployed. In fact, they are regarded as being in a state of nonwork because of the absence of regular wages.

Jung reasoned that if artists deny themselves as laborers, then it is hard to valorize their time and labor into exchange value. He identified this exclusion as a structural problem that, in his opinion, renders artists prone to exploitation:

> Artists can be seen as laborers. If we do not apply the concept of work to artists' work—what I mean is that the concept of artists' labor is important [for changing the perception about artists]. We should not separate arts from work. As I have said before, our senior artists made the mistake of separating arts from work, arts from politics, and arts from a society. It has been a history of separation. I think if we do not overcome this, the future is not bright. . . . There exists a structural problem. The problem is not that artists are directly exploited by capitalists. Rather, artists are already in the game, but the industry is monopolizing the entire field. The music industry and the cultural industry are all joint ventures of the media and capital. They are sucking everything dry.[27]

In this respect, one of the missions of the HCASC is to achieve recognition for artistic activities as labor so as to valorize their economic value. This marks a stark contrast between the HCAC and the HCASC: the former had asserted the exclusiveness of the arts (culture) from economic rationality, while the latter now calls for a fair assessment of the economic value of arts (culture). Thus, the HCASC has penetrated the duality of value—namely, the economic value and the cultural value yielded by artistic (cultural) activities.

Jung's argument that an artist should be regarded as a laborer highlights the ambiguities about culture as end-products. Value can be seen as the worth to someone as well as the worth of something. Cultural goods or services articulate the price of their use benefit in economic terms. Yet they also have distinctive qualities that make them public goods, or different from other private goods. Therefore, the producers of cultural goods and services in fact supply to "a dual market" that, according to an economist's view, comprises "a physical market for the good which determines its economic price, and a market for ideas which determines the good's cultural price."[28] Jung's reasoning implies that while the value of a cultural price is not clear-cut, the worth of the work that supplies goods to a physical market should at least be economically acknowledged.

The urge to regard artists as laborers reveals how impoverishment among the self-employed or freelancers is seen as their own responsibility. The blame is theirs in the absence of wage earning. Doing arts and culture as a full-time job is not seen as proper work but as neglecting one's duties in life. Faring badly as an artist thus deserves no sympathy. Defining artists as laborers unveils how Hongdae actors try to justify the worth of the arts by adapting the labor theory of value. Like Karl Marx, who asserts the value of labor in order to articulate justice and welfare and yet reduces the concept of value to labor,[29] Jung reduces the value of arts to labor. It is, however, a temporary and strategic action in order to articulate the well-being of artists and to avoid being seen as an irresponsible self.

Cho is a self-claimed artist who sees the artist as a loner/laborer/artist. In contrast, Jung is a self-claimed laborer who refuses to identify himself as an artist so that he may pursue the arts. Whether as an artist or a laborer, both acknowledge their precarious livelihoods and seek ways to make a living.

Becoming Makers

Choi, the former CCA representative, shared with me that he had persistently tried to integrate cultural and economic production.[30] At the time of our interview in 2016, Choi had left Hongdae and was supervising cultural projects in the regional cities. He recounted that when he arrived in Hongdae for the first time in 2000, he had tried to create an "urban foreshore." While leading a cultural movement for small-scale shops in Insadong in Seoul, Choi witnessed the limitations of governmental cultural policy, which motivated him to explore grassroots movements when he came to Hongdae. He saw the potential in Hongdae dance clubs to become an urban foreshore—that is, an "ecological environment where concrete places, relations, and activities would endogenously emerge and integrate with each other."[31] He believed that the expansion of the dance club scene would create an urban foreshore where new forms of culture, community, and economy would coevolve.

The topic of "framework" emerged as Choi shared his strategies on how to enrich the Hongdae foreshore. Choi remarked that "place marketing" was a means to achieve his goal of creating the urban foreshore:

> I discerned that this new concept called place marketing would be an advantageous means to pursue my goal, considering my relationship with the city government, which wanted to promote a local economy. I made the best use of this concept. But it did not convey my experiences in city making that much. I had an economically radical perspective. Whether people recognized it or not, I determined to make an alternative economic system. My idea about ecology was embedded in an economically leftist perspective. I projected this nuance onto the notion of place marketing.[32]

Choi's comment about place marketing conforms to the analysis made in Chapter 4 on the manner in which the 2000 Hongdae place-marketing report couched criticisms of capitalism within the framework of urban managerialism. I continued to explore this topic during our interview by asking Choi whether a strategic framework had in effect limited the pursuit of his goal. He replied by acknowledging that if he had had better acumen at that time, he would have focused on the concepts of "place" and "network" rather than place marketing.

> Choi: If I had had better discernment at that time, I would rather have focused on the concept of place and network. If that had happened, I would have come up with alternative ways to tackle the goal. . . .
>
> Me: Maybe place marketing reflected the spirit of the times. It had to catch on at that time. . . .
>
> Choi: How to market Hongdae was a very attractive topic to the authorities. Also, internally, people wanted to pursue their own interests by utilizing this concept. Both interlocked.[33]

Choi concluded that his goal to generate an endogenous urban ecology in Hongdae had failed. As the club scene prospered, the club owners wanted to extend their businesses beyond Hongdae, while external capital and people also wanted to come to Hongdae. Choi shared that he inhibited "human's intrinsic desire for expansion by saying don't do that and don't do this." He, "as a CEO," had "failed to generate new managerial schemes." He further acknowledged that he had failed to cope with the digitization of music production, consumption, and distribution, all of which have changed the role of a place—that of the club—in nurturing an urban ecology.[34]

Choi also revealed that his engagement in Hongdae's club scene led him to conclude that "an endogenous local development is an impossible project." He located this impossibility within the workings of capitalism:

> Segmentation has already begun. But I tried to regress this ongoing trend, which of course did not work. I organized a new festival to create an impactful pivot to unite scattered clubs. But it failed. After that, the productivity of the club scene decreased, and profits were not reinvested for reproduction. Yet each club used money to look after itself instead of reinvesting to develop co-programs. Since then, I came to view the endogenous development of a locality as impossible. I started contemplating the issue of place. . . . I came to give up the idea of the village and determined not to do anything related to village making. Already the village has been fragmented, and life conditions have all been integrated into the market structure. We, embedded in this structure, are too far away from determining our life directions.[35]

Choi explained that the "village," as a place where everyday life takes place, has been integrated into the market. He saw market rules in operation everywhere. This hinders the development of an alternative place with alternative life conditions. Such perspectives, including his notion of the ecology, shed light on his materialistic understanding about culture—in terms of how economic life conditions and substructures determine the sociocultural spheres.

Is it possible to create alternative economic conditions? Choi approached this issue from the perspective of public funds:

> Now, young people have nothing. Everything is blocked. But people have to stimulate their lives and create something. I am not talking about finding jobs. I don't think the markets would find jobs for them. Young people strive to come up with stories to narrate their lives. The markets will use their stories and calculate their money value. In this neoliberal structure, capitalization has been driving people to limitless competition. Without breaking this structure, it is impossible [to create something new]. How can we break this structure? I think the only way is to use public funds. With this

money, we start from creating something small and then create new ecologies for young people. And then they make their own markets. To some extent, the old-fashioned critical mind is still valid. How can we create and consume our culture by ourselves? When we were poor, when I look back at my childhood, the so-called accumulation of capital in the village was not that visible. People managed to get by. Neighbors fed hungry children. I think if we pursue this kind of stuff, something would be possible.[36]

Choi is basically proposing to make new markets with public money. By referring to a poor yet cooperative neighborhood economy of the past, Choi highlights solidarity and self-help. With solidarity at its core, he proposes a new role of the citizen as maker. Our interview hints at the notion of the maker—an individual who creates a cooperative lifestyle by making an alternative market operated by nonmarket rationality:

The concept conveys making one's own life, sharing it with others, and thereby creating culture. If this happens widely, then it would be possible for us to build new ways of making a living. . . . There were more than five hundred people working in the Hongdae clubs. It was a large number. These people used to hold get-togethers in the restaurant. There were discussions about starting a cooperative restaurant where these people could come and eat. The realization of this idea would have completed the construction of a self-sufficient club economy. I should have completed it, but I was not able to. I was soaked in nightlife for a while. Having stopped the fight [to establish a self-sufficient club economy], I became idle, fell into so-called habitual behavior. That was my mistake.[37]

Choi's recent interview reveals the changing themes at the core of his strategies in the last fifteen years. When he established the CCA back in 2003, Choi advocated governance, public-private partnership, and intervention. After the HCD project's cancelation, he spotlighted individual desire as the driving force of culture. He now calls for public funds and solidarity as essential to the creation of a new culture and life conditions. The shift in emphasis from public-mindedness to individual desire and then back to public-mindedness appears to have come full circle. Yet the trajectories of the two public-minded outlooks differ significantly: the earlier notion is closer to public-private partnership, while the later notion addresses socioeconomic solidarity among citizens.

Cho has been a self-claimed artist, Jung claims to be a laborer, and Choi has always been engaged in culture as an economic leftist. Yet each of them has one thing in common: they criticize the limitations of the current workings of capitalism and seek to come up with alternatives in making a livelihood. Cho imagines new working conditions where a loner/laborer/artist is equitably compensated for his or her genuine labor. Meanwhile, Jung asserts the indivisible and fair economic valorization of artists' work. Finally, Choi claims that heightened public-mindedness and solidarity could mitigate the negative impact of unbridled competition posed by contemporary capitalism. However, none of these actors are optimistic. Instead, they appear doubtful about the prospects of making an immediate breakthrough despite having started pursuing alternativeness from their respective positions.

Becoming Entrepreneurs

Sung, an indie musician based in Hongdae since the 1990s, demonstrates how making a living by doing indie music should be seen as a statement of alternativeness in itself.[38] He has been a member of 3rd Line Butterfly, a well-known first-generation indie band. He is also a poet, a lecturer, and a columnist.

Sung divides musicians in Hongdae into two groups—namely, the indie group that has performed music since the 1990s and the new, younger group. According to Sung, indie in the 1990s denoted "the deconstruction of and self-reflection about inflexibility and goal-orientedness."[39] Inflexibility and goal-orientedness seem to refer to the legacy of the totalitarian and militaristic regimes that had operated Korea for over forty years since the Korean War. During our interview, Sung noted that although people thought of indie as an attitude devoid of any goal or intention, he believes deconstruction itself was the goal. He elaborated that "indie people" tried to deconstruct the overwhelming trend of inflexibility and goal-orientedness, as they wanted to construct something better. However, the younger generation, according to him, has the mentality of not wanting to pursue anything. To this generation, in his opinion, the old indie group may appear to be exercising adultism, even when the old group sympathizes with the younger generation. The younger generation, he told me, may regard the effort not to exercise adultism itself as exercising adultism. Sung remarked that he sees it as his challenge to pursue something, including making music and mentoring the younger generation, without revealing its purposefulness.[40]

How is the effortless pursuit of something without revealing its purposefulness related to living in the times of the current capitalism? Sung understands it as about vetoing a neoliberal lifestyle:

> In the 1990s, we were young, and doing music was fun. We indulged in music and did not think about the future. A bit funny, though, at that time, parents paid living expenses for indie musicians. It is only now that indie musicians have to earn money to continue music. . . . To some extent, we could say that now is the heyday of the indie scene, because we are demonstrating one way of living through this society. In this competition-oriented and winner-takes-all total system, indie musicians do their best not to hurt music, like throwing our lives into saving music. Of course, we owe our lives to music, but protecting music itself is to demonstrate an attitude for life. Doing indie music is like refusing to get on the fast bus of neoliberalism and instead walking on an uncertain road. It is like repudiating a mainstream lifestyle, refusing to be concerned with how much monthly salary one earns and where one lives.[41]

His expression, "the heyday of the indie scene," paradoxically spotlights the challenge indie musicians face today—not hurting music but selling enough music to make a living.

What does Sung mean by "not hurting music"? It seems to imply a refusal to conform to market rationality and a unilateral life choice, which the current capitalistic society pushes individuals to adopt. He said that the current music industry does not nurture the creativity of musicians but instead makes them part of corporations. The industry is testing musicians and dumping "the useless." The music industry, he said, forces musicians to become a component of the big corporate world, and if they refuse, the corporations threaten to keep them out of the industry. He believes that the industry makes musicians "hostages":

> If new music emerges, the industry does not allow it to grow or allow musicians to establish their own styles and territories. If, let's say, musicians are worth a thousand dollars at the current stage, companies make a contract of five thousand dollars for advance sales. Then the companies make them part of the corporations and dump away some of them who are evaluated as not profitable. It is how the music industry works. Smart musicians especially are to some extent driven into this kind of situation. . . . The companies fix

the styles of musicians to make salable music. I think, in the extreme case, this would lead to the end of our future. Musicians become hostages of the corporations.[42]

Sung is especially critical of audition shows because he thinks they function as capitalist propaganda. In these shows, K-pop stars and star managers behave like chaebols (conglomerates), treating talented young people and musicians as work-wooers hoping to be picked by the corporations. Those who pass the auditions squirm and cry or jump for joy when the heads of the entertainment establishments choose them. The shows propagate the demands of the capitalists as the correct answer for achieving success:

> Nowadays, propaganda works differently from the previous efforts that coerced people to memorize the Charter of National Education [an outline of national education goals adopted in 1968]. Audition shows educate the demands of capitalists. They are propaganda. So-called K-pop stars Park Jinyoung [CEO of JYI Entertainment] and Yang Hyunsuk [CEO of YG Entertainment] are like chaebols. They are like the heads of Samsung and Hyundae sitting at job interviews. Some pass the interview, and others don't. Every week, audiences watch on TV how these audition candidates struggle to succeed, squirm, fail, and cry. Watching young participants is fun. At the same time, it shows the model answers about how to survive in this society. It is way more effective than reading out the Charter of National Education ten thousand times over. When it is imprinted in the young hearts, they would just want to find favor with the capitalists, without caring for others, and enter the monopolized system. This attitude is an implicit recommendation to the young, and the media propagates it. The media is a servant of the system.[43]

Sung's description of audition shows reads like a means of social control to make a "one-dimensional"[44] society, where mass media instills conformity into individuals thereby stabilizing capitalism.

Sung explained the national craze for audition shows as the result of limited channels for musicians to introduce their music to the public. Because of this limitation, some musicians began to market, circulate, and sell their own music in the early 2000s. He gave examples of his own band, 3rd Line Butterfly, and another band, Crying Nut, as cases of musicians who undertook planning, production, and management of their music.

He said that they might be seen as "entrepreneurs" in the sense that they have been responsible for creating and exploring both new products and markets independent from a few big corporations.[45] The younger generation, however, has become heavily dependent on entertainment corporations because they have come to regard the auditions held by the corporations as their only channel to advertise their music.

Sung is sympathetic to the younger musicians. He said that their livelihoods have become tougher to the extent that having a purpose has become extravagant, pretentious, and unrealistic. Under such circumstances, he feels that a senior musician like himself should demonstrate hope by remaining in the village—that is, Hongdae:

> I am now doing music as a way of living through everyday life, . . . not like an agitated indie musician during the 1990s . . . without looking too shabby or grungy. If I appear like that, younger ones might feel bitter and decide to give up music. If we seniors make a living by doing music and staying in this village [Hongdae], then we might be able to show hope to them.[46]

He associates doing music with continuously throwing small stones at the huge competitive system. He likens those people who throw small stones at the system to a secret society:

> Even though the other party is doing something wrong, if we throw a big rock at the party, it is seen as violence, not as a protest. Therefore, we need to be cautious about it. So we need to place small stones, like tap-tap-tap. This is not as effective as airing audition shows to millions of people. But small cracks may be imprinted in people. Then we might be able to make cracks on such a huge competition system. . . . If we live our every day with this attitude, someday we will die. Then let it be. It is all about this attitude. Now doing music is the same as living everyday life.[47]

My interview with Sung illustrates how musicians in Hongdae have directly experienced the workings of capitalism amid postindustrial economic restructuring in Seoul. The liberalization of the media industry in Korea took place between the 1980s and the 1990s, when conglomerates came to own the broadcasting and media companies. After the 1997 financial crisis, many conglomerates landed heavily in debt, and venture capital surged into the culture and media industries to reorganize them. As a result, a handful of corporations now run the industry, exerting a monopolistic influence on the production and circulation of cultural content. This has been strengthened by the development of the Internet and information technology. Under such conditions, as Sung observes, a limited number of corporations exert their influence on musicians as if the latter were hostages.

Cha, a freelance music critic and short-term contract employee of a venture company, critiques the uniform mass culture and lifestyles provided by some of the corporations. He describes them as "horror-movie-like realities"—where one lives in an apartment built by Samsung, shops in a supermarket stocked by Samsung, works in one of the many Samsung companies, watches TV programs aired by Samsung, and surfs the Internet via a portal site provided by Samsung.[48] Cha, however, acknowledges the difficulties in pursuing alternativeness and becoming a totally new type of a person rather than a flexible laborer in the corporate world. Cha admits that he had become an entrepreneur already in the sense that he has been running his enterprise as a freelance critic in order to make his living. He knew that his current work condition was precarious and his job would soon disappear. He felt that he was like a soon-to-be-extinct dinosaur watching other dinosaurs perish yet not knowing what to do except wait his turn.

Cha questions whether pursuing an alternative lifestyle is about drinking fair-trade coffee in a Hongdae café while listening to indie music. His own answer is that it would only be a different consumption style, a different taste. He notes that many other people in Hongdae, including himself, have been aware of an acute irony: the pursuit of alternativeness in the form of cultural expression is just an expression of aesthetic consumption. He describes himself as a "capitalistic individual" who likes individualism, liberalism, and self-care.[49] However, he told me that he has become concerned about ethics because the question of how to live with others has become more important than ever:

> I do not intend to start a revolution, but I can comment on what is going on now. I am largely contented. But there is a moment when I can't sweep things under the carpet anymore. Now is the time when power or capital is really penetrating everywhere. Every individual is affected by this penetration. In this situation, the question of how to live seems to be even more important than before. Ethical values have become really important more than anything else. Ethics is different from public order. It is now needed so people do not to prey on others.[50]

Cha highlighted that Hongdae has given Korean society a love and a hatred toward capitalism: it has given us sophisticated culture as well as doubt about the unbearable lightness of culture. While he does not propose any revolution or drastic reformation, he emphasizes the establishment of a new set of ethics to lead a virtuous life so as not to hurt one another in the current competition-driven world. Sung and Cha call themselves entrepreneurs, which are similar to a self-responsible agency. Yet they are alert to self-responsibility as a socialization force under the current capitalistic order. They wish to accumulate capital, without hurting music and other people, in addition to pursuing self-care. In this respect, they are like ethical entrepreneurs concerned with moral questions of work and society and caring for the welfare of others.

Labor, Not Culture

The HCD project, although unexecuted, showcases the incorporation of artistic critiques on capitalism into social engineering. The so-called liberal and leftist researchers and cultural activists attempted to take advantage of governmental aspirations for postindustrial restructuring in order to empower subcultural actors. They twisted the notion of place marketing, originally a business and management concept, to serve as an urban governance concept that would nurture local economy by leveraging cultural authenticity. They argued that if the authenticity of the Hongdae scenes could be protected from standardization, their marketplace competitiveness would remain strong. They reasoned that with market competitiveness, a local cultural scene would sustain itself. In this respect, the policy project was proposed to nurture local cultural businesses. Choi admitted that he lacked the discernment to frame his economically leftist perspective. The adaptation of place marketing for leftist cultural politics thus resulted in the intermingling of the "artistic critique" and the "social critique" of capitalism.[51]

The artistic critique puts forward the standardization and commodification of human beings under rationalistic workings of capitalism, while the social critique is more concerned with social inequality and a profit-seeking market economy. These two streams of critiques still remain as the context for the resistance and activism against capitalism. The artistic critique emphasizes authenticity, subjectivity, and liberalization of individuals as a rejection of the totalitarian rationalization and standardization. In contrast, the social critique posits itself as a critique of individualism, accusing the pursuit of unlimited self-interest as an immoral and exploitive bourgeois ideology.[52] The policy ideas underpinning the Hongdae project adopted the artistic critique that human creativity and cultural authenticity should be protected against standardizing market forces. However, it was pitched in the framework of place marketing, which packaged a place as a product. Authenticity makes a subcultural place cool, thus differentiating it from uncool places. Ultimately, what was argued was product differentiation—a main force driving market competitiveness and consumer capitalism.[53]

Hongdae is where countercultural movements and leftist cultural activism first emerged in Korea. It is also where, over the last two decades, the modification of such resistant activism into a business model and a social engineering project first took place. In other words, Hongdae has witnessed the processes of turning individual freedom and creativity—the corrective forces against standardization and commodification—into the essence of market competitiveness, thereby turning political activities into market behaviors. Meanwhile, cultural workers and artists in Hongdae have had to come to terms with new notions of labor, capitalism, and ethics.

Since I embarked on this research in the early 2000s, my interlocutors have at times been resentful, ambitious, and bewildered. Throughout the journey of becoming natives, prosumers, intermediaries, laborers, makers, and entrepreneurs, Hongdae actors have observed the conversion of self-statements, social ideals, and political values into commodities. They have also witnessed the process through which the critiques on capitalism and corrective activism spurred social engineering in ways that are more favorable to capitalism. The people with whom I have interacted might not have communicated with each other for a long time. They used to fight and accuse each other of being self-centered artists and doctrinaire leftists. However, if they were to read this book, they might view themselves as comrades who survived an ironic moment in history. The journey to seek new socioeconomic roles and subjectivities epitomizes the adaptation to living through post-Fordist Seoul, where desirable workers-cum-citizens are seen as akin to artists who produce new creations by investing their whole selves into their works and as entrepreneurs who manage the self and organizations undertaking self-responsibility. My interlocutors did not sound optimistic about becoming ethical entrepreneurs who could change the rules of the system. Yet they are searching for ways to live through and/or live with this capitalism while refusing to become part of the twin forces of consumer capitalism and the marketization of governance.

Conclusion

Entrepreneurial Seoulite

While exploring articles about dance clubs in Hongdae, I came across a magazine article published in 1937 titled "Allow Dance Halls in Seoul."[1] The department head of a record company, a female supervisor of a coffeehouse, and a bar waitress, as well as actresses and *gisaengs* (often translated as Korean geishas), publicly entreated a chief police official to legalize Seoul's dance hall businesses. They insisted that dance halls were places that fostered the emergence of "healthy entertainment culture":

> We have been to Tokyo, Shanghai, and Harbin. Some of us have been to the West. We have observed that Tokyo, Kobe, and Yokohama in Japan, and Beijing, Dairen, and Shenyang in China have healthy entertainment culture thanks to dance halls. We are so envious of them. All the cities in the Empire of Japan as well as all the civilized cities in Asia have dance halls. But only in Seoul, dance halls are not allowed. It is indeed deplorable. . . .
>
> [To the chief police official:] Are you worried that the dancers in dance halls might lure young people into decadence? If so, why have you allowed so many cafés to produce drunkards, and why have you licensed prostitution? If one falls into decadence because of dancing, then this person will be so whatever he or she does.
>
> Stubborn old people and ethicists who are ignorant of the spirit of the times might argue that permitting dance halls results in a waste of "money" in addition to the spread of demoralization. As far as we are concerned, however, these people lack sense. We know that people of Joseon [the kingdom that lasted from 1392 to 1897;

renamed the Korean Empire in 1897] go to restaurants like Myong-wolgwan and Sikdowon [where *gisaengs* provided entertainment services] for socialization. One has to spend at least 40 to 50 *won* for entertainment expenses. However, with one ticket that costs 5 or 10 chon [one hundredth of a *won*], one can enjoy a pleasant night-time. Isn't it more economical and cultured than becoming drunk, wasting health and money eventually?[2]

The petitioners constituted the so-called creative class of their time. They worked in the culture industry, ran trendy urban amenities, and were hailed as the "modern girls and modern boys" in colonial Seoul.[3] They roamed across the cities in Asia and the West, conducting comparative global urbanism wherever they went. They distinguished Joeson people from modern people and healthy entertainment culture from unhealthy overconsumption. They demanded the right to enjoy the modern lifestyles that they observed were prevalent in other parts of the world. In so doing, they self-reflected, explained the status quo, and engaged with others. At the particular juncture where enlightenment, capitalism, urbanization, and colonization were enmeshed with modernization, the dance hall became one of many life spaces where people contemplated about new realities and the (new) spirit of the times.

These "modern" girls and boys in Seoul's dance halls in 1937 are the forerunners of the natives and prosumers in present-day Hongdae. Indeed, contemporary Hongdae cultural workers and artists adopted either the protective self (natives) or the reformist self (prosumers) based on the confrontational framework—cultural vis-à-vis commercial—that defined Hongdae culture. Remarkably, though, both natives and prosumers sought liberation. Natives asserted liberation from depersonalization under capitalism, and prosumers pursued liberation from fragmentization under the same force. In this respect, natives upheld the division between culture and economy while prosumers sought their integration. It is intriguing that the dance halls in both the 1930s and the 2000s became sites where demands for new lifestyles emerged and brought people face to face with the (new) spirit of their times. These comparative observations are closely related to the overarching question that this book pursues: To what extent does Hongdae culture inform Seoul's urbanism in an era where post-Fordist transformations are enmeshed with post-financial-crisis realities?

Cho, the former HCAC representative, has tirelessly reiterated throughout numerous interviews with me that Hongdae is the only place in Korea where the arts can evade the forces of capitalism. Ironically, he has also emphasized that Hongdae is the one place where capitalism thrives most. How should this puzzle be understood? I explain this contradiction by examining Hongdae culture as cultural goods and services that possess both cultural and economic value. The implication of the duality of value has penetrated the debate on whether dance clubs are cultural or commercial places. Chapter 1 details Hongdae culture as a commodity under the continuous process of cultural and economic value making. Cafés, clubs, and shops signify the objectified value, or Hongdae-ness. As market distinctiveness, Hongdae-ness differentiates Hongdae clubs, shops, and cafés from those available in other localities. It creates new value in various markets, such as real estate and tourism. The conversion of any resource into commodities, including those not previously treated as commodities, is seen as the "core procedure of capitalism."[4] Such interconvertibility directs virtually everything toward monetized exchange and organizes the intersection of structures via monetized exchange.[5]

The duality of value and the consequent dilemma of valuation are embedded in the way cultural institutions (referring to legislation, policy, and administrative apparatuses) think and operate. The spirit of capitalism is inscribed in various institutions including rational ideas. Such ideas reconfigure existing social meanings, form a new economic agency, and shape a particular lifestyle.[6] Legal terms and policy ideas are social languages through which individuals encounter the spirit of capitalism and in which they describe themselves and their world. Questions remain as to how people "perform" these ideas. Therefore, I explore how particular ideas inscribed in cultural policy frame socialization processes as well as how various actors articulate, mobilize, and appropriate policy ideas to self-reflect, explain the status quo, and foster social relations. Chapter 2 analyzes the policy ideas embedded in the HCD project in conjunction with the cultural turn in Korea. The discussion details how the project, initially aimed to support subcultural business establishments, had evolved to disseminate the subjectivity of desirable workers and citizens.

A post-Fordist society prioritizes "the conception of goods—the immaterial domain" over the actual making of goods for profit generation.[7] In this sense, post-Fordist economies are seen as "culturalized," and these culturalized economies are led by the "revolution in information and organization," which distinguishes them from the previous revolutions led by the innovations of machines (i.e., steam engines) and energy (i.e., electricity).[8] The previous Fordist economies incorporated wage workers into the production system and combined the economic concern of productivity with the social concern of the welfare of individual workers.[9] This work organization was dismantled with the advancement of the culturalized industrial revolution, which prompted the flattening of hierarchical working organizations, the emergence of flexible working and outsourcing, the horizontal delegation of responsibility, and the increased accountability for one's performance.[10]

As elaborated in the previous chapters, the cultural turn in Seoul coincided with the efforts to liberate Korea from a regulatory and militant state and with attempts at economic recovery in the aftermath of the 1997 Asian financial crisis. The financial crisis and crisis management are understood as part of the global expansion of neoliberalism, which set in motion social transformations in Korea. Such areas of transformation spanned economic restructuring, family, youth, womanhood, labor, and social welfare. In particular, Jesook Song has noted the integration of democratization movements with economic neoliberalization under the presidency of Kim Dae Jung.[11] Kyung-Sup Chang has observed the convergence of state developmentalism and neoliberal reforms during the period of financial crisis management.[12] Both scholars note an accelerated shift from developmental regimes to neoliberal regimes as a significant impact of the Asian financial crisis. In other words, they have highlighted Korea's pathway toward neoliberalization, which was conditioned by the financial crisis.

The chorus of a song that aired repeatedly in the lead-up to the 1988 Summer Olympics in Seoul remains imprinted on my memory: "Our one year is equivalent to ten years of the world. Let's advance towards the world and the future." Koreans condensed ten years of world history into a single year; indeed, a decade appeared long enough for Koreans to experience an epochal transition. Within ten years, from Korea's democratization in 1987 to the financial crisis in 1997, living in a democratic welfare society became an obsolete project. Massive restructuring occurred, and the nation had to undergo a creative destruction.

Relatively insufficient scholarly attention, however, has been paid to how the economic crisis affected the cultural domain, and vice versa, as well as how the cultural turn affected the formulation of the times. At the historical juncture when the economic temporalities of the financial crisis and the political temporalities of democratization movements were enmeshed, creativity/culture became an elective affinity, connecting one project aimed at pursuing a liberalized civil society with another aimed at spurring economic restructuring. This has resulted in the treatment of creativity/culture as a force for social liberalization, a focal point for politics against globalization, and an engine for the knowledge-oriented industries. Creativity/culture has become an ethos guiding how one should engage with the new realities. This explains why Hongdae became a site where cultural activism was integrated into social engineering by advocating the artist as a national champion and an epitome of the enterprising self.

The exploration of the enterprising self from a structural perspective comprises one of the goals of this book. The other goal is to examine the subjective experience of encountering the enterprising self. Recent research on Korean culture approaches the K-wave phenomenon from the perspectives of cultural consumption, media analysis, and cultural management and policy. Meanwhile, studies on Seoul have centered on its transformation as a global, creative city. Rather than examining the K-wave or the city itself, I choose to explore the experience of living through the city-in-transition. Chapters 3, 4, and 5 present and analyze my interview materials collected in Seoul for over a decade. These data, though inevitably partial, reveal what it means to live through post-financial-crisis Seoul from the perspective of artists and cultural workers. The cultural turn is now in decline, and it goes hand in hand with the labor turn. These chapters examine the period immediately after the zenith of the cultural turn, focusing on the confusion of artists and cultural workers as they attempt to grasp what happened. Put differently, these chapters portray a time lag: they cover the decade during which my interlocutors were initially riding the high tide and then subject to the ebb and flow of the cultural moment.

In particular, Chapters 4 and 5 detail the struggles and challenges of seeking new socioeconomic roles faced by cultural subjects. Zygmunt Bauman highlights that cities are now forced to treat urbanism as a local issue even though it is a globally conceived and formed reality.[13] Likewise, the Hongdae project drove people to find cultural and local solutions to noncultural national and global quandaries that have informed Seoul's urbanism. The project, though never executed, led individuals in Hongdae to interpret and explain socioeconomic realities in cultural terms and to seek individual solutions to structural problems. They were encouraged to think of themselves as "place imagineers" and "cultural engineers" who could save Hongdae from megastores, franchise outlets, and real estate developers. Overall, their efforts revealed the responsibilization inscribed in the enterprising self.

It was a striking moment when the representative of the newly established HCASC denied the members' identity as artists and instead claimed they were laborers. Hongdae people observed that artists began to develop new self-technologies to survive—by continuously mastering the self to cope with uncertainty of the market. Refusing the label "artist" and instead choosing to be a "person doing arts," whether as a passive or symbolic gesture, made me view becoming a laborer as a corrective force against both the enterprising self and a uniform lifestyle conducive to the capitalist order. Yet this self-making process is nonetheless self-contradictory. It conflates art with labor; it justifies the worth of the arts by adopting a work ethic. The work ethic as a disciplinary force might confine individuals within a process of perpetual work, thereby making them *animal laborans*, or animals of labor.[14] Becoming a laborer in order to do art, ironically, negates the self as an artist.

Becoming a laborer is, however, a temporary and strategic action one might take to avoid misrepresentation as one type of artist—the irresponsible self (unemployed and idle)—and/or the enforced representation as another type—the entrepreneurial self (self-organizing and self-sufficient). Likewise, during my most recent round of field research, my interlocutors expressed their wishes not to be misrepresented and were keen to correct any inaccurate portrayal. Their actions demonstrate an effort to identify a language that better describes the status quo and the workings of self-reflexivity regarding the socialization forces and subjectification processes to which they have been exposed.

Bauman quotes from Italo Calvino's novel *Invisible Cities* in a bid to contemplate self-reflexivity as a way to living in an uncertain era:[15] The inferno of the living is what is already here, rather than something that will happen. The way to escape from the inferno therefore lies either in becoming part of it so as not to see it, or in learning to recognize who and what do not constitute the inferno so as help them survive. The former offers the easier and more popularly chosen way. In contrast, the latter demands permanent alertness and anxiety and is thus chosen by fewer people. Chapter 5 examines those Hongdae people who have chosen to be alert and anxious in embracing uncertainty. They are uncertain about the future of Hongdae as well as their own livelihoods. Yet they have been trying to discern who and what they should not become. They refuse to become hostages of the corporations. They identify with neither artists as the irresponsible self nor artists as the forces of consumer capitalism. Yet they wish to sell music, enough to make a living, without hurting music.

In the spring of 2018, I convened a seminar on Hongdae culture in Seoul. A handful of people came, including university students, an artist, and cultural planners. All were in their twenties and thirties. When I described prosumers and natives, the participants exclaimed that they knew who they were. They pointed out that prosumers and natives comprised only a part of Hongdae. I felt the participants' uneasiness, even anger, toward the protagonists in my research. One participant said, "They were just fighting for becoming a neighborhood bully." The artist commented that "scholars" and "the older generation" feel pity for artists although they do not deserve sympathy. We did not talk about Hongdae culture. Instead, we discussed what was "wrongly" informed about Hongdae and the minimum wage system. I harbored mixed feelings after the seminar. It felt as if I had been taken to task for being a complacent scholar. I felt like a miserable Generation Xer who has been worn down by the struggle for survival and did not even notice that she had become a grown-up. I felt embarrassed. Emphasizing culture to these young people was like an evasion of the responsibilities of a grown-up.

Previously, Hongdae culture was invoked to reify particular urban lifestyles. Such aspired lifestyles were described as part of "a free-spirited neighborhood" in the tourist guidebooks as well as enforced as "a community of play, culture, and economy" in policy documents.[16] Then people condensed diverse subject matters into Hongdae culture—including freedom, cultural politics, community, the creative industries, and urban ecology. Today, however, people invoke Hongdae culture in reference to work, ethics, and capitalism. Ideals for making artisan coffee or becoming makers might constitute the enterprising self disguised as work ethic. Yet people care about how to make a good business out of a good culture. They are more concerned with the ethics of capitalism than the ethics of work. By articulating ethics, people try to integrate value as price with value as pricelessness and forge symbioses between entertainment houses and independent labels, renters and tenants, and artisan coffee and franchise coffee. They demand the right or at least the option to continue to be freelancers, self-employed, and tenants.

People try to get a better sense of what actually concerns them and what they really want to do with their lives. They assert alternativeness in making a living instead of making alternative culture. Like the representative of the HCASC, people have begun to cross off unwanted or wrongly placed labels that have been stuck on them. In so doing, Hongdae culture has been deconstructed. To what extent, then, does Hongdae culture inform the post-financial-crisis urbanism of Seoul? People seek the ethics of capitalism to sustain Hongdae culture as one possible yet seemingly difficult way of life in Seoul—making a living by selling good music, good coffee, and good designs, in one's own shop as an artist, an artisan, and an ethical entrepreneur. Not in a megamall as a part-time worker.

Notes

INTRODUCTION

1. U-jin Ch'a, "Toshi gyehoek kwa hongdae-ap indissin: Wae 1996 nyŏnin'ga?" [Urban planning and indie scene of Hongdae area: Why 1996?], P'üllaetp'om [Platform], no. 45 (2014): 68–73; Hongdae Cultural Studies Network and Seokyo Arts Experiment Center, Hongdaeap munhwayesul saengt'aegye hwalsŏnghwarŭl wihan chŏngch'aekyŏn'gugwaje [A study of the policy for the activation of the culture and art ecosystem in Hongdae area] (Seoul: Seoul Foundation for Arts and Culture, 2014); Sooah Kim, "Hongdae konggan ŭi munhwajŏk ŭimi pyŏnhwa: Konggan iyongjaŭi kiŏkŭl chungsimŭro" [Changes in the cultural meaning of the Hongdae place: With focus on the memories of place users], Midiŏ, Chendŏ wa Munhwa [Media, Gender, and Culture] 30, no. 4 (2015): 83–123.

2. Luc Boltanski and Ève Chiapello, The New Spirit of Capitalism, trans. Gregory Elliott (New York: Verso, 2007), 8.

3. Thomas Lemke, "'The Birth of Bio-politics': Michel Foucault's Lecture at the Collège de France on Neo-liberal Governmentality," Economy and Society 30, no. 2 (2001): 191.

4. Boltanski and Chiapello, The New Spirit of Capitalism, 3.

5. Creative industries refers to those in which products and services contain a substantial element of creative endeavor encompassing the culture industries (or forms of cultural production and consumption with symbolic or expressive elements at their core) as well as many types of research and software development. United Nations, Creative Economy Report, 2013 Special Edition: Widening Local Development Pathways (New York: United Nations Development Program and United Nations Educational, Scientific, and Cultural Organization, 2013), 19, http://www.unesco.org/culture/pdf/creative-economy-report-2013.pdf.

6. Gwanung Chŏng, "Yojŭm chŏlmŭn X-sedaeŭi tŭngjanggwa t'ükching" [The emergence and characteristics of Generation X], MBC News (Seoul), April 5, 1994, http://imnews.imbc.com/20dbnews/history/1994/1926247_19434.html. All translations are mine.

7. Pyŏla Kim, "Chŏngch'unsongga, kŭdŭri taeshin ulmyŏ purŭd" [An ode to youth, they cried out for us], in K'ŭraing nŏt: Kŭdŭri taeshin ulbujitta [Crying Nut: They cried out for us], ed. Sŭngho Chi (Seoul: Outsider, 2002), 206.

8. Cho, interview by the author, Seoul, August 27, 2004. All translations are mine.

9. The Uruguay Round was one of the multilateral trade negotiations under the framework of the General Agreement on Tariffs and Trade (GATT) that led to the creation of the World Trade Organization (WTO).

10. Jisoo Kim, *K'ŭllik! Taejungmunhwa-ga poyŏyo* [Click! Mass culture is seen] (Seoul: Munhwamadang, 1999).

11. Myung-Rae Cho, "Flexible Sociality and the Postmodernity of Seoul," *Korea Journal* 39, no. 3 (1999): 128.

12. Byung Doo Choi, "Shinjayujuŭijŏk tosihwawa kiŏpchuŭi tosi p'ŭrojekt'ŭ" [Neoliberal urbanization and projects of an entrepreneurial city], *Han'gukchiyŏkchirihak'oeji* [Journal of the Economic Geographical Society of Korea] 14, no. 3 (2011): 263–85.

13. Jesook Song, *South Koreans in the Debt Crisis: The Creation of a Neoliberal Welfare Society* (Durham, NC: Duke University Press, 2009).

14. Kunio Saito, "Korea's Economic Adjustments under the IMF-Supported Program," January 21, 1998, https://www.imf.org/external/np/speeches/1998/012198a.pdf.

15. Marshall Berman, *All That Is Solid Melts into Air: The Experience of Modernity* (New York: Verso, 1983).

16. Yŏngju Han et al., *Wŏltŭk'ŏp chŏllyakchiyŏk changsomak'et'ing: Hongdaejiyŏk munhwahwalsŏnghwa pangan* [Place marketing of the (2002) World Cup strategic areas: Schemes for vitalizing culture in Hongdae] (Seoul: Seoul Development Institute, 2000).

17. Ryu, interview by the author, Seoul, February 9, 2004; Ch'a, "Tosi gyehoek kwa hongdae-ap indissin."

18. K-wave, known as *Hallyu* in Korean, refers to the popularity of Korean entertainment and culture across Asia and other parts of the world. See "Hallyu (Korean Wave)," *Korea.net*, http://www.korea.net/AboutKorea/Culture-and-the-Arts/Hallyu (accessed August 24, 2018).

19. "K'ŭllŏptei chungdanŭl t'onghae hongdaeapkwa k'ŭllŏbŭl yaegihada" [Speaking on Hongdae and Hongdae clubs through the discontinuation of Club Day], *Street H*, February 2011, http://street-h.com/magazine/44979.

20. Galina Gornostaeva and Noel Campbell, "The Creative Underclass in the Production of Place: Example of Camden Town in London," *Journal of Urban Affairs* 34, no. 2 (2012): 169–88.

21. "K'ŭllŏptei chungdanŭl t'onghae hongdaeapkwa."

22. Lemke, "'The Birth of Bio-politics,'" 191.

23. Han et al., *Wŏltŭk'ŏp chŏllyakchiyŏk changsomak'et'ing*.

24. Ch'angyŏn Kim, "IMF ihu t'ojishijangbyŏnhwa mit t'ojijŏngch'aek panghyang" [The changes of the land market and the direction of the land policy after the IMF bailout], *Chungbuk Report* 8, no. 1 (2001): 51–58.

25. Il Paek, "IMF ihu han'gukkyŏngje kujobyŏndonggwa taean: Soyu, saengsan, sobiŭi sahoehwawa munhwasobiŭi chŏllyakchŏk sŭnggyŏk" [Structural change of the Korean economy and its alternatives after the IMF bailout: The socialization of possession, production, and consumption, and the strategic elevation of cultural consumption], *Munhwagwahak* [Cultural Science] 43 (2005): 40–68; Byung Doo Choi, "Tosi jutaegsijang-ŭi byeondongseonggwa budongsan jeongchaeg-ŭi han'gye: IMF wigi ihu seo-ul-eul chungsimŭro" [Volatility of the urban housing market and the limitation of real estate policy: Focus on Seoul and the capital area after the IMF crisis], *Han'gukchiyŏkchirihak'oeji* [Journal of the Economic Geographical Society of Korea] 15, no. 1 (2009): 138–60; Dongŭn Yim and Chongbae Kim, *Met'ŭrop'ollisŭ sŏurŭi t'ansaeng:*

Sŏurŭi salmŭl mandŭrŏnaen kwŏllyŏk, chabon, chedo kŭrigo yongmangdŭl [Birth of metropolis Seoul: Power, capital, system that created life in Seoul] (Seoul: Banbi, 2015).

26. Choi, "Tosi jutaegsijang-ŭi byeondongseonggwa budongsan jeongchaeg-ŭi han'gye," 145–46.

27. Han et al., *Wŏltŭkŏp chŏllyakchiyŏk changsomak'et'ing*, 3.

28. Dongŭn Yim, *Sŏuresŏ yumok'agi* [Being a nomad in Seoul] (Seoul: Munhwagwahaksa, 1999).

29. Korea Culture Policy Institute, *Munhwatosi mit munhwabelt'ŭ chosŏngbangan yŏn'gu* [A study on designation and development of the cultural city or cultural belt] (Seoul: Korea Culture Policy Institute, 2000), 1–2.

30. Richard Florida, *The Rise of the Creative Class: And How It's Transforming Work, Leisure, Community and Everyday Life* (New York: Basic Books, 2002); Charles Landry, *The Creative City: A Toolkit for Urban Innovators*, 2nd ed. (London: Earthscan, 2009).

31. Luc Boltanski, "The Left after May 1968 and the Longing for Total Revolution," *Thesis Eleven* 69, no. 1 (2002): 1–20.

32. Boltanski and Chiapello, *The New Spirit of Capitalism*.

33. Jim McGuigan, *Cool Capitalism* (London: Pluto, 2009).

34. Han et al., *Wŏltŭkŏp chŏllyakchiyŏk changsomak'et'ing*, 32–33.

35. Ibid., 11.

36. Ibid., 33.

37. Naomi Klein, *No Logo: Taking Aim at the Brand Bullies* (New York: Picador, 2000), 279.

38. Daniel Miller, "The Uses of Value," *Geoforum* 39, no. 3 (2008): 1122–32.

39. Song, *South Koreans in the Debt Crisis*, 2–9.

40. Huck-Ju Kwon, "Advocacy Coalitions and the Politics of Welfare in Korea after the Economic Crisis," *Policy and Politics* 31, no. 1 (2003): 69–83; Song, *South Koreans in the Debt Crisis*.

41. Paek, "IMF ihu han'gukkyŏngje kujobyŏndonggwa taean"; Choi, "Tosi jutaegsijang-ŭi byeondongseonggwa budongsan jeongchaeg-ŭi han'gye"; Choi, "Shinjayujuŭijŏk Tosihawawa Kiŏpchuŭi Tosi P'ŭrojek'ŭ"; Hyŏn Choi, "Shijangin'ganŭi hyŏngsŏng: Saenghwalsegyeŭi shingminhwawa chŏhang" [Birth of a market person: Colonization and resistance of the lifeworld], *Tonghyanggwa Chŏnmang* [Trend and Prospect] 81 (2011): 156–94.

42. Hŭiyŏn Cho, "Hegemoni kusŏngjŏk kwajŏnggwa 'hegemoni kyunyŏlt': Kukmin, minjung, shiminŭi tonghak" [The process of constructing of hegemony and the "fissure of hegemony": Dynamics of nation, people, and citizen], in *Tongwŏndoen kŭndaehwa: Pak Chŏng-hŭi kaebal tongwŏn ch'eje ŭi chŏngch'i sahoejŏk ijungsŏng* [Mobilized modernization: The political and social duality under Park Jung Hee's developmental mobilization regime] (Seoul: Humanitas, 2010), 331–77; Choi, "Shinjayujuŭijŏk Tosihawawa Kiŏpchuŭi Tosi P'ŭrojekt'ŭ."

43. Sang-u Yun, "IMF wigi ihu shinjayujuŭiŭi naebuhwa kwajŏng" [The internalization process of neoliberalism after the IMF crisis], *Asea yŏn'gu* [Journal of Asiatic Studies] 56, no. 3 (2013): 364–95.

44. Song, *South Koreans in the Debt Crisis*, 10.

45. Jongŭn Chŏng, "Han'guk munhwajŏngch'aegŭi ch'angjojŏk chŏnhoe: Chayu, t'uja, ch'angjosŏng" [The creative turn of Korean cultural policy: Freedom, investment, and creativity], *In'ganyŏn'gu* [Human Studies], no. 25 (2013): 33–71; Wŏn'gyŏng Chŏn,

"Han'guk tŭrama such'ul huwŏnjŏngch'aegŭi hyoyulsŏnge taehan koch'al: 1995–2005 rŭl chungshimŭro" [A study of the efficiencies of Korean drama export support policies: Between 1995 and 2005], *Küllobŏlmunhwak'ont'ench'ŭ* [Global Cultural Content], no. 14 (2014): 153–78.

46. Gabyŏng Chŏng, "Urinara munhwajŏngch'aegŭi inyŏme kwanhan yŏn'gu" [A study on the cultural political ideas in South Korea], *Munhwajŏngch'aengnonch'ong* [Journal of Cultural Policy] 5 (December 1993): 82–132; Yangyŏl O, "Han'gugŭi munhwahaengjŏngch'egye 50 nyŏn: Kujo mit kinŭngŭi pyŏnch'ŏn'gwajŏnggwa kŭ kwaje" [Fifty years of the cultural administration systems in South Korea: The process of transition and its task of structure and function], *Munhwajŏngch'aengnonch'ong* [Journal of Cultural Policy] 7 (1995): 29–74; Kwanghyŏn Sim, "Munminjŏngbuŭi kaehyŏkkwa 90 nyŏndae munhwajŏngch'aegŭi kibon kwaje" [Korean civilian government's reform and the basic task of the cultural policy in the 1990s], *Munhwajŏngch'aengnonch'ong* [Journal of Cultural Policy] 5 (1993): 18–30; Hakswun Yim, "Munhwa sanŏp yŏngyŏkkwa yesuryŏngyŏge taehan chŏngch'aek mokp'yodŭl yangnipkanŭngsŏng yŏn'gu" [A study on the compatibility of policy goals between a cultural policy domain and an art domain], *Munhwajŏngch'aengnonch'ong* [Journal of Cultural Policy] 13 (December 2001): 279–300.

47. Ch'angkyu Kwŏn, "Munhwa'esŏ t'rk'ont'ench'ŭ'ro: Han'guk munhwaŭi sanŏp'wawa hallyuhwarŭl chungshimŭro" [The transition from culture to contents: Focusing on the industrialization of Korean culture and the Korean wave], *Taejungsŏsayŏn'gu* [Journal of Popular Narrative] 20, no. 3 (2014): 221–44.

48. Chŏn, "Han'guk tŭrama such'ul huwŏnjŏngch'aegŭi hyoyulsŏnge taehan koch'al."

49. Marion Fourcade-Gourinchas and Sarah L. Babb, "The Rebirth of the Liberal Creed: Paths to Neoliberalism in Four Countries," *American Journal of Sociology* 108, no. 3 (2002): 535.

50. Max Weber, *The Protestant Ethic and the Spirit of Capitalism*, trans. Stephen Kalberg (London: Routledge, 2010).

51. Anthony Giddens, *Capitalism and Modern Social Theory: An Analysis of the Writings of Marx, Durkheim and Max Weber* (Cambridge: Cambridge University Press, 2011).

52. Marion Fourcade, *Economists and Societies: Discipline and Profession in the United States, Britain, and France, 1890s to 1990s* (Princeton, NJ: Princeton University Press, 2009).

53. Boltanski and Chiapello, *The New Spirit of Capitalism*.

54. Ibid., 20.

55. Luc Boltanski and Ève Chiapello, "The New Spirit of Capitalism" (paper presented at the Conference of Europeanists, Chicago, IL, March 14–16, 2002).

56. Boltanski and Chiapello, *The New Spirit of Capitalism*.

57. Yoshiyuki Sato, *Shin jiyushuhi to kenryoku* [Neoliberalism and power], trans. Kim Sangwun (Seoul: Humanitas, 2014), 50–51.

58. Richard Sennett, "The New Capitalism," *Social Research* 64, no. 2 (1997): 167.

59. McGuigan, *Cool Capitalism*, 160–65.

60. Lemke, "'The Birth of Bio-politics.'"

61. Zygmunt Bauman, *Liquid Times: Living in an Age of Uncertainty* (Cambridge, UK: Polity, 2011).

62. Choi, interview by the author, Seoul, September 3, 2004.

63. Min'gyŏng Kim, "Hongdae wŏnjumindŭrŭi moim 'honghap': Hongdaemunhwa salligo saengjon'gwŏn chik'igo" [Gathering of Hongdae natives "Honghap": Save Hongdae culture and the right to live], *Weekly Donga* (Seoul), February 20, 2004, http://weekly.donga.com/List/3/all/11/73125/1.

64. Merry M. White, *Coffee Life in Japan* (Berkeley: University of California Press, 2012).

65. See Culture and Arts Promotion Act, clause 2, article 3, available at http://www.law.go.kr/법령/문화예술진흥법.

66. Hongdae Culture Academy, "Minutes of the HCA Seminar," February 15, 2006.

67. Jung, interview by the author, Seoul, April 14, 2016.

68. John L. Campbell, "Ideas, Politics, and Public Policy," *Annual Review of Sociology* 28, no. 1 (2002): 21–38; Jean-Pierre Olivier de Sardan, *Anthropology and Development: Understanding Contemporary Social Change*, trans. Antoinette Tidjani Alou (London: Zed Books, 2005); Cris Shore and Susan Wright, "Audit Culture and Anthropology: Neo-liberalism in British Higher Education," *Journal of the Royal Anthropological Institute* 5, no. 4 (1999): 557–75; Cris Shore, Susan Wright, and Davide Però, eds., *Policy Worlds: Anthropology and the Analysis of Contemporary Power* (Oxford: Berghahn Books, 2011); Crispian Fuller, "'Worlds of Justification' in the Politics and Practices of Urban Regeneration," *Environment and Planning D: Society and Space* 30, no. 5 (2012): 913–29.

CHAPTER 1

1. Mapo district is one of twenty-five autonomous districts in Seoul. The district is 23.87 square kilometers, or approximately 3.9 percent the size of Seoul. In 2016 Mapo district's population was 390,887. See Mapo District Office, "Households and Population by Dong (Resident Registration)," 2017, http://www.mapo.go.kr/CmsWeb/resource/image/stat2013/pdf/year2017/3.pdf.

2. Dongjun Yi, "Kyelkwukun kangnamsuthail?" [Finally Gangnam style?], *Street H*, August 2012, http://street-h.com/magazine/45255.

3. Jinae Kim, "Sŏul hongdaep: Koetchadŭrŭi 'yesulch'anggo'. . . 'indi chŏngshin' hwal shiwirŭl tanggyŏra" [Hongdae area in Seoul: "Art storage" of loonies . . . "indie spirit" pulls the bowstring], *Chosun Shinmun* [Chosun Daily News] (Seoul), February 25, 2002.

4. Hyŏnju Yi, "Sobogi," in *Hongdaeap'ŭro wa* [Come to the Hongdae area, Seoul], ed. Dongjun Yi (Seoul: Paibuksŭ, 2005), 118.

5. Kiung Yi, "Chent'ŭrip'ik'eisyŏn hyogwa: Hongdaejiyŏk munhwayuminŭi hŭrŭmgwa taeanjŏk changsoŭi hyŏngsŏng" [Gentrification effects: The flow of cultural refugees and making alternative places in the vicinities of Hongdae], *Tosiyŏn'gu* [City Studies], no. 14 (2015): 67.

6. Mapo District Office, *Mapo District's Guide to the Hongdae Area* (Seoul: Mapo District Office, 2015).

7. U-jin Ch'a, "Toshi gyehoek kwa hongdae-ap indissin: Wae 1996 nyŏnin'ga?" [Urban planning and indie scene of Hongdae area: Why 1996?], *P'ŭllaetp'om* [Platform], no. 45 (2014): 68–73; Yŏngju Han et al., *Wŏltŭk'ŏp chŏllyakchiyŏk changsomak'e'ing: Hongdaejiyŏk munhwahwalsŏnghwa pangan* [Place marketing of the (2002) World Cup

strategic areas: Schemes for vitalizing culture in Hongdae] (Seoul: Seoul Development Institute, 2000); Hongdae Cultural Studies Network and Seokyo Arts Experiment Center, *Hongdaeap munhwayesul saengt'aegye hwalsŏnghwarŭl wihan chŏngch'aek-yŏn'gugwaje* [A study of the policy for the activation of the culture and art ecosystem in Hongdae area] (Seoul: Seoul Foundation for Arts and Culture, 2014); Sooah Kim, "Hongdae konggan ŭi munhwajŏk ŭimi pyŏnhwa: Konggan iyongjaŭi kiŏkŭl chungsimŭro" [Changes in the cultural meaning of the Hongdae place: With focus on the memories of place users], *Midiŏ, Chendŏ wa Munhwa* [Media, Gender, and Culture] 30, no. 4 (2015): 83–123.

8. Hongik Environmental Development Institution, *Hongdae munhwajigu t'adangsŏng chosa mit kwalligyehoek suribyŏn'gua* [Feasibility study on the Hongdae cultural district and administration plan] (Seoul: Hongik Environmental Development Institution, 2004).

9. Club Culture Association, *K'ŭllŏmmunhwa* [Club culture] (Seoul: Club Culture Association, 2004); Ch'a, "Toshi gyehoek kwa hongdae-ap indissin"; Hongik Environmental Development Institution, *Hongdae munhwajigu t'adangsŏng chosa*; Muyong Lee, "The Place Marketing Strategy and the Cultural Politics of Space: A Case of the Club Cultures at the Hongdae Area in Seoul" (Ph.D. diss., Seoul National University, 2003); Han et al., *Wŏltŭk'ŏp chŏllyakchiyŏk changsomae'ing*.

10. Jonghwi Kim, preface to *Narara baendeu ttwieora indi* [Fly bands, run indie], ed. An Iyŏngno et al., 4–25 (Seoul: Hanaem, 2000); Hyunjoon Shin, "Rokŭmakkwa 'ŏlt'ŭ undong'" [Rock music and the "alt-movement"], *Munhwagwahak* [Cultural Science], no. 9 (1996): 175–80.

11. Sooah Kim, *Sŏulshi munhwagongganŭi tamnonjŏk kusŏng: Hongdae kongganŭl chungshimŭro* [Discursive structure of the cultural space in Seoul: Focused on Hongdae area] (Seoul: Seoul Institute, 2013); Hongdae Cultural Studies Network and Seokyo Arts Experiment Center, *Hongdaeap munhwayesul saengt'aegye hwalsŏnghwarŭl.*

12. For example, there were 50 clubs, 92 publishing companies, 219 studios, 11 bookshops, 102 art academies, 20 art shops, 7 record shops, 46 craft shops, and 2 ceramic shops. Hongik Environmental Development Institution, *Hongdae munhwajigu t'adangsŏng chosa*, 10.

13. Hongdae Cultural Studies Network and Seokyo Arts Experiment Center, *Hongdaeap munhwayesul saengt'aegye hwalsŏnghwarŭl*, 4.

14. Examples of these books include Dongjun Yi, *Hongdaeap'ŭro wa* [Come to the Hongdae area, Seoul] (Seoul: Paibuksŭ, 2006); 21 segi-chŏnmangtong'in [A coterie for looking at the twenty-first century], *Hongdaeap kŭmyoil* [Friday night in Hongdae area] (Seoul: Manu, 2007); Han'gukshirhŏmyesulchŏngshin [Korea Performance Art Spirit], *Segye shirhŏmyesurŭi mek'a hongdaeap* [Mecca of experimental art in the world, Hongdae area) (Seoul: Symposium, 2009); Gi-Wan Sung, *Hongdaeap saebyŏk se shi: Sŏnggiwanŭi indimunhwa rimiksŭ* [Three a.m. in Hongdae: Sung Gi-Wan's indie culture remix] (Seoul: Samunnanjŏk, 2009); Soyŏng Yang, *Hongdaeap twitkolmok: Ŏnŭ t'ŭraendŭset'ŏŭi hongdaeap k'ap'e kaidŭ* [Backstreets of Hongdae area: Café guide to Hongdae area] (Seoul: Kŭrigoch'aek, 2009); Mapo District Office, *Hongdaeap ch'omch'om kaidŭ: Hongdaeap soksoktŭri chŭlgigi* [Hongdae area guide: Enjoy everything in the Hongdae area] (Seoul: Mapo District Office, 2010); Aejin Kim, *Chigŭmŭn Hongdae sŭt'ail: 101 kaji chŭlgŏumi kadŭk'an kot* [Now is Hongdae style: 101 places full of joy] (Seoul: Ungjinthinkbig, 2012); Chinsŏk Yang, *Hongdaeap'esŏ changsahamnida: Nadaun*

kagero sŏnggonghan kolmoksajang 9 inŭi pigyŏl [Doing business in Hongdae area: The secret of nine shop owners who achieved shops with personality] (Seoul: Sosobooks, 2015); Mapo desainch'ulp'anchinhŭngjiguhyŏbŭihoe [Mapo Design and Publication Promotion Association], *Hongdaeap tijaint'pch'ulp'an chido* [Design and publication map of Hongdae area] (Seoul: Propaganda, 2015); and Blue Ribbon Survey, *Hongdae matchip 427* [Delicious restaurants in Hongdae area 427] (Seoul: BRmedia, 2016).

15. "Hot Nights at Hongdae's Hottest Clubs," *VisitSeoul.net*, January 3, 2016, http://english.visitseoul.net/tours/Hot-Nights-at-Hongdae's-HottestClubs_/579; "Seoul-ui bam -eul jeulgija: Hongdae ildae, gyeonglidan gil" [Let's enjoy a Seoul night: Hongdae area], *VisitSeoul.net*, December 26, 2015, http://korean.visitseoul.net/tours/서울의-밤을-즐기자-홍대-일대-경리단-길_/56.

16. David Bell and Mark Jayne, eds., *City of Quarters: Urban Villages in the Contemporary City* (Aldershot, UK: Ashgate, 2004); David Harvey, *The Condition of Postmodernity: An Enquiry into the Origins of Cultural Change* (Oxford: Blackwell, 1989); Scott Lash and John Urry, *Economies of Signs and Space* (London: Sage, 1994); John Urry, *Consuming Places* (London: Routledge, 1995); Sharon Zukin, *Loft Living: Culture and Capital in Urban Change* (New Brunswick, NJ: Rutgers University Press, 1989).

17. Trevor Barnes and Thomas A. Hutton, "Situating the New Economy: Contingencies of Regeneration and Dislocation in Vancouver's Inner City," *Urban Studies* 46, no. 5–6 (2009): 1254; Thomas A. Hutton, *The New Economy of the Inner City: Restructuring, Regeneration and Dislocation in the Twenty-First Century Metropolis* (New York: Routledge, 2009).

18. Hongik Environmental Development Institution, *Hongdae munhwajigu t'adangsŏng chosa*, 4.

19. Mihye Cho, "Mapping the Hong-Dae Area in Seoul: A New and Unstable Economic Space?" in *New Economic Spaces in Asian Cities: From Industrial Restructuring to the Cultural Turn*, ed. Peter W. Daniels, K. C. Ho, and Thomas A. Hutton (London: Routledge, 2012), 133–49.

20. Ch'a, "Toshi gyehoek kwa hongdae-ap indissin."

21. Kyŏnghwa Yim, "Hongdaeap'ŭn pudongsanŏpso chŏnjaengtŏ?" [Is Hongdae area the battlefield of real estate?], *Street H*, May 2014, http://street-h.com/magazine/81370.

22. Ara Cho, "Sŏulshi kesŭt'ŭhausŭ Hongdaeap 158 kot, 1 wi" [Hongdae area guesthouse 158, top of Seoul], *Street H*, March 2015, http://street-h.com/magazine/89037.

23. Kyŏnghwa Yim, "Masŭi kyŏngyŏnjang hongdaeap" [The competition venue of taste, Hongdae area], *Street H*, November 2014, http://street-h.com/magazine/82530.

24. Kyŏnghwa Yim, "Hongdaeap p'aesyŏnsyop" [Fashion shops of Hongdae area], *Street H*, October 2014, http://street-h.com/magazine/81420.

25. Kyŏnghwa Yim, "Pom. Hongdaeap. Kolmokk'ap'e!" [Spring. Hongdae area. Café alley!], *Street H*, February 2015, http://street-h.com/magazine/88882.

26. Dean MacCannell, *The Tourist: A New Theory of the Leisure Class*, rev. ed. (Berkeley: University of California Press, 1989).

27. Yŏngmi Yi, "Chŏngnyŏnmunhwanŭn wae hap'il 1970 nyŏndae yŏssŭlkka?" [Why did youth culture emerge in the 1970s?], *Inmulgwasasang* [Person and Idea] 214 (February 2016): 168–81.

28. Ŭnyŏng Song, "1960–70 nyŏndae han'gugŭi taejungsahoehwawa taejungmunhwaŭi chŏngch'ijŏng ŭimi" [The process of becoming mass society and the political meaning of popular culture in 1960s–1970s Korea], *Sanghŏhakpo* [Journal of Korean

Modern Literature] 32 (June 2011): 187–226; Yŏngmi Yi, "Han'gung taejunggayosaŭi tongnyŏkkwa sedae kan yangshik, ch'wihyang kaltŭng" [Dynamics of Korean pop history and differences of style and taste among the generations], *Taejungŭmak* [Korean Journal of Popular Music] 11 (May 2013): 33–69.

29. Hyunjoon Shin, "Han'gung p'abŭi 'kŏnch'uk'ak'ŭl wihayŏr Idonghanŭn sŏurŭi ŭmakchŏng changsodŭl, 1976–1992" [A contribution to the construction of Korean pop: Popular music and places in mobile Seoul, 1976–1992], *SAI* 14 (2013): 610.

30. Ibid.

31. Sangpong Yi, "Modŏn p'ok'ŭ amagi 80 nyŏndae han'guktaejungŭmage mich'in yŏnghyange kwanhan yŏn'gu" [A study about the influence of '80s Korean folk music on popular music] (master's thesis, Dankook University, 2010).

32. Jakka Kim, "'K'auntŏ kŏlch'ŏ' ka sarajin hongdaeap" [Hongdae area, where "counter culture" disappeared], *Kyunghyang Shinmun* [Kyunghyang Daily News] (Seoul), September 30, 2014, http://news.khan.co.kr/kh_news/khan_art_view.html?code=990100& artid=201409302130075.

33. Kim, preface to *Narara baendeu ttwieora indi*; Lee, "The Place Marketing Strategy and the Cultural Politics of Space."

34. Han et al., *Wŏltŭk'ŏp chŏllyakchiyŏk changsomak'et'ing*; Ch'a, "Toshi gyehoek kwa hongdae-ap indissin."

35. Jakka Kim, "Why: Hongdaeap indibaendeuui sijag-eun . . ." [Why: The beginning of Hongdae indie bands . . .], *Chosun Shinmun* [Chosun Daily News] (Seoul), March 14, 2008, http://newsplus.chosun.com/site/data/html_dir/2010/03/11/2010031101867.html; Shin, "Rokŭmakkwa 'ŏlt'ŭ undong."

36. Ch'a, "Toshi gyehoek kwa hongdae-ap indissin."

37. Hongik Environmental Development Institution, *Hongdae munhwajigu t'adang-sŏng chosa.*

38. Han et al., *Wŏltŭk'ŏp chŏllyakchiyŏk changsomak'et'ing.*

39. Lee, "The Place Marketing Strategy and the Cultural Politics of Space," 130.

40. Ibid.

41. Hongik Environmental Development Institution, *Hongdae munhwajigu t'adang-sŏng chosa.*

42. "K'ŭllŏptei chungdanŭl t'onghae hongdaeapkwa k'ŭllŏbŭl yaegihada" [Speaking on Hongdae area and Hongdae clubs through the discontinuation of Club Day], *Street H*, February 2011, http://street-h.com/magazine/44979.

43. Choi, interview by the author, Seoul, December 24, 2003.

44. Kim, email correspondence with the author, December 28, 2003.

45. For more on the so-called deculturalization of Hongdae culture caused by the proliferation of dance clubs, see Juhyŏn Yi, "Hongdaeap 20 nyŏn, kŭ munhwajŏk shirhŏmdŭ" [20 years of Hongdae, its cultural experiments], *Hankoyreh 21* (Seoul), November 7, 2002, http://h21.hani.co.kr/arti/special/special_general/6522.html; Juhyŏn Yi, "Hongdaeap, it'aewŏn ttaragana" [Is Hongdae following Itaewon?], *Hankoyreh 21* (Seoul), November 7, 2002, http://h21.hani.co.kr/arti/cover/cover_general/6528.html; Hyesŏng Yu, "Hongdaeap·shinch'on 'munhwa' ŭi wigi: P'at'imunhwae hwidullin a, uriŭi 'hongdaeap'!" [Crisis of "culture" of Hongdae and Shinchon: Our "Hongdae" bossed around by party culture!], *Weekly Hankook* (Seoul), June 23, 2004, http://weekly .hankooki.com/lpage/cover/200406/wk2004062311420237040.htm; Kim Yunjong, "Hong-daeap = indimunhwa mek'a t'oesaek" [Tarnishing Hongdae area = indie mecca], *Donga*

Daily (Seoul), August 6, 2005, http://news.donga.com/3/all/20050806/8216791/1; Gogŭm Kim, "Hongdaeap kŭllŏp, puhwarinya, mollaginya: 'Pulp'yŏngdŭng kongyŏnbŏbŭro kosa wigi' chiptan panbal" [Hongdae clubs, revival or collapse: Group resistance of the crisis of the decline by "unequal performance act"], *Munhwa Daily* (Seoul), July 22, 2006, http://www.munhwa.com/news/view.html?no=2006072201030130073024; Sanghun Yi, "T'oep'yee tchotkyŏnan indimunhwat . . . hongdaeam 'sunsu' rŭl ilt'a" [Indie culture expelled by decadence . . . Hongdae lost "innocence"], *Kyunghyang Shinmun* [Kyunghyang Daily News] (Seoul), October 30, 2006, http://news.khan.co.kr/kh_news/khan_art_view.html?code=940100&artid=200610301829401; Hojin Nam, "Pul kkŏjyŏganŭn sŏul hongdaeap raibŭk'ŭllŏp" [Dimming Hongdae live clubs in Seoul], *Kyunghyang Shinmun* [Kyunghyang Daily News] (Seoul), November 19, 2006, http://news.khan.co.kr/kh_news/khan_art_view.html?code=210000&artid=200611191650271; and Hanul U, "Hongdaeap, sunsuyesul chigo sangŏpchŏng taensŭk'ŭllŏm ttŭgo" [Hongdae area, falling-down arts and coming-up commercial dance clubs], *Segye Daily* (Seoul), February 19, 2004, http://www.segye.com/newsView/20040218001104.

46. Kim, "Hongdaeap = indimunhwa mek'a t'oesaek."

47. Lee, "The Place Marketing Strategy and the Cultural Politics of Space"; Han et al., *Wŏltŭkŏp chŏllyakchiyŏk changsomak'et'ing.*

48. Lee, "The Place Marketing Strategy and the Cultural Politics of Space."

49. "K'ŭllŏptei chungdanŭl t'onghae hongdaeapkwa."

50. Internet café bulletin board, 2004 (site discontinued; accessed December 2, 2004).

51. Han et al., *Wŏltŭkŏp chŏllyakchiyŏk changsomak'et'ing.*

52. Ryu, interview by the author, Seoul, October 11, 2003.

53. 54th Club Day poster made by CCA, October 28, 2005.

54. Suryŏn Pak and Haeyong Son, "'Hongdaeap munhwa' ka tansok taesang?" [Is "Hongdae culture" a target of crackdown?], *JoongAng Daily* (Seoul), August 3, 2005, http://news.joins.com/article/1649587; Muyong Lee, "The Landscape of Club Culture and Identity Politics: Focusing on the Club Culture in the Hongdae Area of Seoul," *Korea Journal* 44, no. 3 (2004): 65–107.

55. I saw this map when I was conducting field research in 2004. Although it is not clear when it was produced, the map was created in preparation of the 2002 World Cup. Theaters, performing organizations, galleries, exhibition places, art shops, and festival agencies were labeled "cultural space"; the Fringe Festival, Korea Experimental Arts Festival, and Hongdae Street Art were labeled "cultural event."

56. Hyunjoon Shin and Pil Ho Kim, "Birth, Death, and Resurrection of Group Sound Rock," in *Korean Popular Culture Reader*, ed. Kyung Hyun Kim and Youngmin Choe (Durham, NC: Duke University Press, 2014), 275–95.

57. Ibid.; Hyunjoon Shin, *Kayo, k'eip'ap kŭrigo kŭnŏmŏ: Han'guk taejungŭmakŭl ingnŭn munhwajŏk p'ŭrijŭm* [Popular song, K-pop and beyond: Cultural prism for reading Korean popular music] (Seoul: Tolbegae, 2013).

58. Giwan Sung (band musician), interview by the author, Seoul, April 13, 2016; Munshik Jung (band musician), interview by the author, Seoul, April 14, 2016.

59. Choi, interview by the author, Seoul, April 16, 2016.

60. Sung, interview by the author.

61. Chŏng, interview by the author, Seoul, October 9, 2004.

62. Lee, "The Place Marketing Strategy and the Cultural Politics of Space," 180.

63. Chŏng, interview by the author.

64. Sŭnghyŏng Yi, "Chayu, kaesŏng, chabonŭi 'kongjon' shirhŏm" [Experimenting with the "coexistence" of freedom, idiosyncrasy, and capital], *Munhwa Daily* (Seoul), August 26, 2003, http://www.munhwa.com/news/view.html?no=200308260101193003 0002.

65. Ibid.

66. See the Free Market website, at http://www.freemarket.or.kr/?page_id=4485.

67. Yun, interview by the author, Seoul, January 19, 2004.

68. Accessory seller, interview by the author, Seoul, January 19, 2004.

69. Hyesŏng Yu, "Hongdaeap·shinch'on 'munhwa' ŭi wigi."

70. Ibid.

71. Cho, interview by the author, Seoul, August 27, 2004.

72. Hong, interview by the author, Seoul, August 26, 2004.

73. Mapo District Office, *Hangout in Hongdae* (Seoul: Mapo District Office, 2013).

74. This information comes from various issues of *Street H* published between 2014 and 2016. *Street H* is a community magazine published by Jang Sung Whan, who has lived in Hongdae since the 1980s. The monthly magazine, in print since 2009, features information on local events, businesses, and people.

75. Ŭnsŏn Yim, "Mokkong, tto tarŭn kamsusŏngŭi ch'urhyŏn" [Woodworking, the emergence of another sensitivity], *Street H*, May 2016, http://street-h.com/magazine/93694.

76. Jinsŏg Yang, "Changsaga yesurida" [Business is art], *Street H*, August 2014, http://street-h.com/magazine/45409.

77. Jiyŏn Chŏng, "Paul Avril: Kŭdŭrŭi konggani kunggŭmhada" [Paul Avril: Curious about their spaces], *Street H*, June 2013, http://street-h.com/magazine/45237.

78. This observation is based on the content of interviews featured in *Street H* between 2012 and 2016.

79. Ssamzie Space, *Ssamzie Space Journal 1*, vol. 9, *Ssamzie Art Book* (Seoul: Ssamzie Space, 2000), 25. "Furious kids" refers to young people, especially emerging young artists at that time.

80. Sinae Gang, "Chaseytay noli kongkan 'Pokhapmwunhwakhaphey,'" [Next generation play space, "multicultural café"], *Goodtimezine*, April 2006.

81. Ko, interview by the author, Seoul, September 20, 2004.

82. Gabi Cho, "Pinbŭradŏsŭ: Kŏp'iŭi Aputŏ Zkkaji mannal su innŭn kot pinbŭradŏsŭ" [Bean Brothers: Factory-type café where you can taste the A to Z of coffee], *Street H*, August 2014, http://street-h.com/magazine/81041.

83. Jongyun Kim, "Hongdaeap'e shinsedae p'aesyŏnhaeng" [New generation fashion street in Hongdae area], *JoongAng Daily* (Seoul), April 21, 1995, http://news.joins.com/article/3051860.

84. Hyemin Pak, "Kam chabatta, t'rnŭkkimp'yot' k'aejuŏl" [Sensed it, "!" casual], *JoongAng Daily* (Seoul), November 8, 2002, http://news.joins.com/article/4375241.

85. Yi, "Kyelkwukun kangnamsuthail?"

86. Ibid.

87. Mapo District Office, *Hangout in Hongdae*.

88. Mapo District Office, *Mapo District's Guide*.

89. Untitled Seoul Culture Foundation brochure, 2014.

90. Mapo District Office, *Mapo District's Guide*.

91. Mapo District Office, *Hangout in Hongdae*.

92. Seoul Culture Foundation, *Brochure of Seoul Culture Foundation*.

93. Jiyŏn Chŏng, "Khapheyka chwuek sokulo kelewassta: Pihaintu censi" [Café strolling down memory lane: Behind exhibition], *Street H*, April 2013, http://street-h.com/magazine/45387.

94. Cihyen Yi, "3 Sam Partners: Kongkanul nemesen khaphey" [3 Sam Partners: Beyond just a café], *Street H*, January 2014, http://street-h.com/magazine/45597.

95. Merry M. White, *Coffee Life in Japan* (Berkeley: University of California Press, 2012).

96. William H. Sewell, Jr., "A Theory of Structure: Duality, Agency, and Transformation," *American Journal of Sociology* 98, no.1 (1992): 29.

97. Ibid.

98. Daniel Miller, "The Uses of Value," *Geoforum* 39, no. 3 (2008): 1122.

CHAPTER 2

1. Yŏngju Han et al., *Wŏltŭkŏp chŏllyakchiyŏk changsomak'et'ing: Hongdaejiyŏk munhwahwalsŏnghwa pangan* [Place marketing of the (2002) World Cup strategic areas: Schemes for vitalizing culture in Hongdae] (Seoul: Seoul Development Institute, 2000).

2. Jesook Song, *South Koreans in the Debt Crisis: The Creation of a Neoliberal Welfare Society* (Durham, NC: Duke University Press, 2009).

3. Ibid., 2.

4. Ibid., 14.

5. Such municipal visions include Seoul Metropolitan Government, *Shijŏngunyŏn 4kaenyŏn kyehoek: 2006–2010 (makko maeryŏginnŭn segyedoshi Seoul)* [Municipal administrative 4-year planning: 2006–2010 (clear and charming world city Seoul)] (Seoul: Seoul Metropolitan Government, 2009), http://www.riss.kr/search/detail/DetailView.do?p_mat_type=d7345961987b50bf&control_no=bb4c6e02944f2f89ffeobdc3ef48d419#redirect. The vision aimed to transform Seoul into the financial, cultural, economic, and business hub of East Asia.

6. The 2020 urban plan for Seoul, presented in 2006, envisioned Seoul as "the world-cultural city" and "the central city of Northeast Asia." See Seoul Metropolitan Government, *2020 Seoul City Basic Urban Plan* (Seoul: Seoul Metropolitan Government, 2006), 17, http://urban.seoul.go.kr/4DUPIS/download/sub3_1_old/1_seoul_basic.pdf.

7. Presented in 2005, the district government's administrative principle, "The 21st-Century Mapo Vision," aimed to enhance quality of life and local competitiveness.

8. Norman Long, "Exploring Local/Global Transformations: A View from Anthropology," in *Anthropology, Development and Modernities: Exploring Discourses, Counter-tendencies and Violence*, eds. Alberto Arce and Norman Long (London: Routledge, 2000), 184–201; Jean-Pierre Olivier de Sardan, *Anthropology and Development: Understanding Contemporary Social Change*, trans. Antoinette Tidjani Alou (London: Zed Books, 2005).

9. John L. Campbell, "Ideas, Politics, and Public Policy," *Annual Review of Sociology* 28, no. 1 (2002): 21–38; Crispian Fuller, "'Worlds of Justification' in the Politics and Practices of Urban Regeneration," *Environment and Planning D: Society and Space* 30, no. 5 (2012): 913–29; Olivier de Sardan, *Anthropology and Development*; Cris Shore and

Susan Wright, "Audit Culture and Anthropology: Neo-liberalism in British Higher Education," *Journal of the Royal Anthropological Institute* 5, no. 4 (1999): 557–75.

10. Jim McGuigan, *Culture and the Public Sphere* (London: Routledge, 1996), 1.

11. Raymond Williams, *Keywords: A Vocabulary of Culture and Society* (London: Fontana, 1976).

12. Geir Vestheim, "Instrumental Cultural Policy in Scandinavian Countries: A Critical Historical Perspective," *European Journal of Cultural Policy* 1, no. 1 (1994): 57–71.

13. Sunpok Sŏ, "Munhwayesulchinhŭngbŏbŭi naeyongbunsŏkkwa hwan'gyŏngbyŏnhwae ttarŭn ippŏppanghyang" [Analysis of the culture and arts promotion act and legislative direction by environmental change], *Munhwajŏngch'aengnonchong* [Journal of Cultural Policy] 18 (February 2007): 69–100.

14. Inmunk'ont'ench'ŭhak'oe [Human Contents Academy], *Munhwak'ont'ench'ŭ immun* [Introduction to cultural contents] (Seoul: Bookkorea, 2006).

15. Young-Jeong Pak, "Historical Distinctiveness of Korean Cultural Policy: Present and Future" (paper presented at the 2016 International Conference on Cultural Policy Research, Seoul, July 6, 2016).

16. Ministry of Culture and Tourism, *2002 munhwajŏngch'aekpaeksŏ* [2002 cultural policy white paper] (Seoul: Ministry of Culture and Tourism, 2003); Gabyŏng Chŏng, "Urinara munhwajŏngch'aegŭi inyŏme kwanhan yŏn'gu" [A study on cultural political ideas in South Korea], *Munhwajŏngch'aengnonch'ong* [Journal of Cultural Policy] 5 (December 1993): 82–132.

17. David Hesmondhalgh and Andy C. Pratt, "Cultural Industries and Cultural Policy," *International Journal of Cultural Policy* 11, no. 1 (2005): 7.

18. Pak, "Historical Distinctiveness of Korean Cultural Policy."

19. Chŏng, "Urinara munhwajŏngch'aegŭi inyŏme kwanhan yŏn'gu."

20. Jongŭn Chŏng, "Han'guk munhwajŏngch'aegŭi ch'angjojŏk chŏnhoe: Chayu, t'uja, ch'angjosŏng" [The creative turn of Korean cultural policy: Freedom, investment, and creativity], *In'ganyŏn'gu* [Human Studies], no. 25 (2013): 39.

21. Ibid.

22. Ministry of Culture and Tourism, *Munhwaganguk (C-Korea) 2010: Munhwaro puganghago haengbok'an taehanmin'gugŭi miraejŏllyak* [The cultural power (C-Korea) 2010: The future strategies for wealthy and happy Korea through culture] (Seoul: Ministry of Culture and Tourism, 2005).

23. Chŏng, "Urinara munhwajŏngch'aegŭi inyŏme kwanhan yŏn'gu"; Yangyŏl O, "Han'gugŭi munhwahaengjŏngch'egye 50 nyŏn: Kujo mit kinŭngŭi pyŏnch'ŏn'gwajŏnggwa kŭ kwaje" [Fifty years of the cultural administration systems in South Korea: The process of transition and its task of structure and function], *Munhwajŏngch'aengnonch'ong* [Journal of Cultural Policy] 7 (December 1995): 29–74; Kwanghyŏn Sim, "Munminjŏngbuŭi kaehyŏkkwa 90 nyŏndae munhwajŏngch'aegŭi kibon kwaje" [Korean civilian government's reform and the basic task of the cultural policy in the 1990s], *Munhwajŏngch'aengnonch'ong* [Journal of Cultural Policy] 5 (1993): 18–30; Hakswun Yim, "Munhwa sanŏp yŏngyŏkkwa yesuryŏngyŏge taehan chŏngch'aek mokp'yodŭl yangnipkanŭngsŏng yŏn'gu" [A study on the compatibility of policy goals between a cultural policy domain and an art domain], *Munhwajŏngch'aengnonch'ong* [Journal of Cultural Policy] 13 (December 2001): 279–300.

24. Huck-Ju Kwon, "Advocacy Coalitions and the Politics of Welfare in Korea after the Economic Crisis," *Policy and Politics* 31, no. 1 (2003): 69–83.

25. Song, *South Koreans in the Debt Crisis*, 3.

26. Ibid., 6.

27. Il Paek, "IMF ihu han'gukkyŏngje kujobyŏndonggwa taean: Soyu, saengsan, sobiŭi sahoehwawa munhwasobiŭi chŏllyakchŏk sŭnggyŏk" [Structural change of the Korean economy and its alternatives after the IMF bailout: The socialization of possession, production, and consumption, and the strategic elevation of cultural consumption], *Munhwagwahak* [Cultural Science] 43 (September 2005): 40–68; Byung Doo Choi, "Tosi jutaegsijang-ŭi byeondongseonggwa budongsan jeongchaeg-ŭi han'gye: IMF wigi ihu seo-ul-eul chungsimŭro" [Volatility of the urban housing market and the limitation of real estate policy: Focused on Seoul and the capital area after the IMF crisis], *Han'gukchiyŏkchirihak'oeji* [Journal of the Economic Geographical Society of Korea] 15, no. 1 (2009): 138–60.

28. Sang-u Yun, "IMF wigi ihu shinjayujuŭiŭi naebuhwa kwajŏng" [The internalization process of neoliberalism after the IMF crisis], *Asea yŏn'gu* [Journal of Asiatic Studies] 56, no. 3 (2013): 364–95.

29. Song, *South Koreans in the Debt Crisis*, 10.

30. Ibid.

31. Ibid., 2.

32. Wŏn'gyŏng Chŏn, "Han'guk tŭrama such'ul huwŏnjŏngch'aegŭi hyoyulsŏnge taehan koch'al: 1995–2005 rŭl chungshimŭro" [A study for the efficiencies of Korean drama export support policies: Between 1995 and 2005], *Kŭllobŏlmunhwak'ont'ench'ŭ* [Global Cultural Content], no. 14 (2014): 153–78.

33. A similar observation on Asia has been made, where authentic culture has been emphasized as uniqueness for gaining a competitive edge in the global market as well as projecting a self-image to the rest of the world. See Brenda S. A. Yeoh, "The Global Cultural City? Spatial Imagineering and Politics in the (Multi)Cultural Marketplaces of South-East Asia," *Urban Studies* 42, no. 5–6 (2005): 945–58; and Ananya Roy and Aihwa Ong, eds., *Worlding Cities: Asian Experiments and the Art of Being Global* (Oxford: Wiley-Blackwell, 2011).

34. Korea Culture Policy Institute, *Munhwajŏngch'esŏng hwangnibŭl wihan chŏngch'aekpangan yŏn'gu* [A study on the policy measures for establishing cultural identity] (Seoul: Korea Culture Policy Institute, 2002), 5, 283.

35. Chŏngsu Kim, "Yech'ŭkpulga'ŭi mihak: Hallyuesŏ paeunŭn munhwajŏngch'aegŭi kyohun" [The beauty of the unpredictability: Cultural policy lessons of the Korean wave] (paper presented at the Seoul Association for Public Administration International Conference, Seoul, October 27, 2006); Yim, "Munhwa sanŏp yŏngyŏkkwa yesuryŏngyŏge."

36. Yŏnghwa Choi, "Yi myŏngngbak chŏngbuŭi kiŏpkukka p'ŭrojekt'ŭrosŏ hallyujŏngch'aek: Chŏllyakkwan'gyejŏk chŏpkŭnbŏbŭl t'onghan kujowa chŏllyak punsŏk" [The Korean wave policy as a corporate-state project of the Lee government: The analysis of structures and strategies based on the strategic-relational approach], *Kyŏngjewa Sahoe* [Economy and Society], no. 97 (2013): 252–85; Chŏng, "Han'guk munhwajŏngch'aegŭi ch'angjojŏk chŏnhoe"; Chŏn, "Han'guk tŭrama such'ul huwŏnjŏngch'aegŭi hyoyulsŏnge taehan koch'al"; Pyŏngmin Yi, "Ch'amyŏjŏngbu munhwasanŏpchŏngch'aegŭi p'yŏnggawa hyanghu chŏngch'aekpanghyang" [An evaluation of cultural industry policies in Korean participatory government and future policy perspectives], *Inmunk'ont'ench'ŭ* [Humanities Content] 9 (June 2007): 205–35.

37. Ministry of Culture and Tourism, *Munhwagangguk (C-Korea)* 2010, 1; see also Korea Tourism Organization, *2010 munhwagangguk (C-Korea 2010) yuksŏngjŏllyak* [Strategy for C-Korea 2010] (Seoul: Korea Tourism Organization, 2005).

38. Ministry of Culture and Tourism, *2009 munhwajŏngch'aekpaeksŏ* [2009 cultural policy white paper] (Seoul: Ministry of Culture and Tourism, 2010).

39. Ministry of Culture, Sports and Tourism, *2014 munhwajŏngch'aekpaeksŏ* [2014 cultural policy white paper] (Seoul: Ministry of Culture, Sports and Tourism, 2015), 31.

40. Choi, "Yi myŏngngbak chŏngbuŭi kiŏpkukka p'ŭrojekt'ŭrosŏ hallyujŏngch'aek"; Ch'angkyu Kwŏn, "Munhwa'esŏ t'rk'ont'ench'ŭ'ro: Han'guk munhwaŭi sanŏp'wawa hallyuhwarŭl chungshimŭro" [The transition from culture to contents: Focusing on the industrialization of Korean culture and the Korean wave], *Taejungsŏsayŏn'gu* [Journal of Popular Narrative] 20, no. 3 (2014): 221–44.

41. Kwŏn, "Munhwa'esŏ t'rk'ont'ench'ŭ'ro," 258.

42. Korea Culture Policy Institute, *Munhwajigu chosŏng modelgaebal mit chŏngch'aekpanghyange kwanhan yŏn'gu* [Research on cultural district development and policy direction] (Seoul: Korea Culture Policy Institute, 1999).

43. Korea Culture Policy Institute, *Munhwatosi mit munhwabelt'ŭ chosŏngbangan yŏn'gu* [A study on designation and development of the cultural city or cultural belt] (Seoul: Korea Culture Policy Institute, 2000), 25.

44. Korea Culture Policy Institute, *Munhwajigu chosŏng modelgaebal*, 27.

45. Yŏnchin Kim, "Munhwajiguŭi munjejŏmgwa kaesŏn panghyang" [Problems of and improvements for the cultural district], *Hwan'gyŏngnonch'ong* [Journal of Environmental Studies] 51 (December 2012): 115–29.

46. Dongŭn Yim, *Sŏuresŏ yumok'agi* [Being a nomad in Seoul] (Seoul: Munhwagwahaksa, 1999).

47. Jongno District Office, *Daehakro munhwajigu kwalligyehoek* [Administrative plan of Daehakro cultural district] (Seoul: Jongno District Office, 2005), 8–9, http://www.sfac.or.kr/artbattery/images/download/%EC%9E%AC%EB%8B%A8%20%EA%B5%AD%EB%AC%B8%20%EB%B8%8C%EB%A1%9C%EC%8A%88%EC%96%B4%202014.pdf.

48. Korea Culture Policy Institute, *Munhwajigu chosŏng modelgaebal*, 25.

49. Korea Culture Policy Institute, *Munhwatosi mit munhwabelt'ŭ chosŏngbangan yŏn'gu*, 1–2.

50. Scholars such as Yŏnchin Kim and Sunpok Sŏ propose to amend this definition to better execute the CD policy. See Kim, "Munhwajiguŭi munjejŏmgwa kaesŏn panghyang"; and Sŏ, "Munhwayesulchinhŭngbŏbŭi naeyongbunsŏkkwa hwan'gyŏngbyŏnhwae ttarŭn ippŏppanghyang."

51. The act was revised in 2016. According to the new definition, cultural facilities refer to places that are continuously used for cultural and artistic activities. They include (1) venues and facilities for performance, (2) exhibition places such as museums and art galleries, (3) libraries, (4) multiuse facilities for performances and other cultural events, and (5) creative spaces where artists perform their activities and exhibit their works and performances.

52. Franco Bianchini and Lia Ghilardi, "The Culture of Neighbourhoods: A European Perspective," in *City of Quarters: Urban Villages in the Contemporary City*, ed. David Bell and Mark Jayne (Aldershot, UK: Ashgate, 2004), 237–48; Lia Ghilardi, "Cultural Planning and Cultural Diversity," in *Differing Diversities: Transversal Study on the Theme*

of Cultural Policy and Cultural Diversity, ed. Tony Bennett (Strasbourg: Council of Europe, 2001), 116–27; Hans Mommaas, "Cultural Clusters and the Post-industrial City: Towards the Remapping of Urban Cultural Policy," *Urban Studies* 41, no. 3 (2004): 507–32.

53. Franco Bianchini, "Cultural Planning in Post-industrial Societies," in *Cultural Planning: Center for Urbanism*, ed. Katrine Østergaard (Copenhagen: Royal Danish Academy of Fine Arts, 2004), 18.

54. Bianchini and Ghilardi, "The Culture of Neighbourhoods," 19.

55. Charles Landry, *The Creative City: A Toolkit for Urban Innovators*, 2nd ed. (London: Earthscan, 2009).

56. Richard Florida, *The Rise of the Creative Class: And How It's Transforming Work, Leisure, Community and Everyday Life* (New York: Basic Books, 2002).

57. Muyong Lee, "The Landscape of Club Culture and Identity Politics: Focusing on the Club Culture in the Hongdae Area of Seoul," *Korea Journal* 44, no. 3 (2004): 65–107.

58. Han et al., *Wŏltŭk'ŏp chŏllyakchiyŏk changsomak'et'ing*, 30.

59. Ibid., 93.

60. Ibid., 104.

61. Ibid., 11.

62. Ibid., 216–17.

63. Ibid., 9–21.

64. Ibid., 116. According to the report, the clubs in Hongdae were categorized as "underground live clubs" and "techno clubs" (47).

65. Ibid., 32, 33.

66. Ibid., 33.

67. Naomi Klein, *No Logo: Taking Aim at the Brand Bullies* (New York: Picador, 2000), 279.

68. Florida, *The Rise of the Creative Class*; Landry, *The Creative City*.

CHAPTER 3

1. Jun Kim, "Sŏul hongdaeap munhwajigu chijŏng" [Hongdae area is demarcated as cultural district], *Kyunghyang Shinmun* (Seoul) [Kyunghyang Daily News], January 11, 2003, http://news.khan.co.kr/kh_news/khan_art_view.html?code=950201&artid=2003 01110055101; Associated News, "Hongdae shinch'on tŭng munhwajigu chijŏngdoenda" [Hongdae and Shinchon will be demarcated as cultural districts], *Hankoyreh 21* (Seoul), September 18, 2003, http://legacy.www.hani.co.kr/section-005000000/2003/09/0050 00000200309181322001.html.

2. Thomas Bierschenk and Jean-Pierre Olivier de Sardan, "ECRIS: Rapid Collective Inquiry for the Identification of Conflicts and Strategic Groups," *Human Organization* 56, no. 2 (1997): 240.

3. Ryu, interview by the author, Seoul, September 2, 2004; Kim, interview by the author, Seoul, October 13, 2004.

4. Kim, email correspondence with the author, December 28, 2003. "Mania" apparently refers to people who like the independent music of Hongdae and possess insider knowledge about clubs and events in the area.

5. I observed the distribution of free cigarette packs during my fieldwork in 2004.

6. Muyong Lee, "The Place Marketing Strategy and the Cultural Politics of Space: A Case of the Club Cultures at the Hongdae Area in Seoul" (Ph.D. diss., Seoul National University, 2003), 354 (emphasis in original).

7. Club Culture Association, *K'üllömmunhwa* [Club culture] (Seoul: Club Culture Association, 2004), 277.

8. Cited in Club Culture Association, *K'üllömmunhwa*, 77.

9. Choi, interview by the author, Seoul, September 3, 2004.

10. Club Culture Association, *K'üllömmunhwa*.

11. Choi, interview by the author.

12. Lee, interview by the author, Seoul, September 2, 2004.

13. Choi, interview by the author.

14. Lee, interview by the author, Seoul, March 6, 2004.

15. Choi and Lee both make this point in my interviews with them.

16. Choi, interview by the author.

17. Ibid.

18. Kim, interview by the author.

19. Ryu, interview by the author.

20. Cho, interview by the author, Seoul, February 15, 2004.

21. Hongdae Culture and Arts Cooperation, "Minutes of the Meeting for the Establishment of the HCAC," January 20, 2004.

22. Hongdae Culture and Arts Cooperation, "Minutes of the HCAC," January 28, 2004.

23. Hongdae Culture and Arts Cooperation, flyer distributed during the opening ceremony of the HCAC, February 19, 2004.

24. Ibid.

25. Söhüi Choi, "Hongdaeap munhwa chik'igi" [Protecting Hongdae culture], *KBS News* (Seoul), February 11, 2004, http://news.kbs.co.kr/news/view.do?ncd=541059.

26. See the Cultural Action home page at http://www.culturalaction.org.

27. Organizer of a cultural event company, interview by the author, Seoul, March 2004.

28. Hongdae Culture and Arts Cooperation, "Minutes of the HCAC," January 20, 2004.

29. Min'gyöng Kim, "Hongdae wönjumindürüi moim 'honghap': Hongdaemunhwa salligo saengjon'gwön chik'igo" [Gathering of Hongdae natives "Honghap": Save Hongdae culture and the right to live], *Weekly Donga* (Seoul), February 20, 2004, http://weekly.donga.com/List/3/all/11/73125/1; see also Cho, telephone interview by the author, Seoul, May 8, 2005.

30. Cho, telephone interview by the author.

31. Lee, interview by the author, March 6, 2004.

32. Cho, interview by the author, Seoul, August 27, 2004.

33. Ibid.

34. Ryu, interview by the author.

35. Ibid.

36. Cho, interview by the author, February 15, 2004.

37. I gleaned this from various interviews and informal conversations during my field research in 2004.

38. Choi, interview by the author, Seoul, September 2, 2004.

39. Quoted in Maŭryŏndae [Community union], *Irŏn maŭresŏ salgoshipta, 2002: Maŭlmandŭlgi paeksŏ* [Want to live in this community, 2002: Community-making white paper] (Seoul: Maŭryŏndae, 2003), 80.
40. Ibid.
41. Choi, interview by the author, September 2, 2004.
42. Ibid.
43. Culture Club Association, *K'ŭllŏmmunhwa*, 77, 81.
44. Cho raised this several times during our interviews conducted over a decade.
45. Cho, interview by the author, August 27, 2004.
46. Kim, interview by the author.
47. Ryu, interview by the author.
48. These observations are drawn from interviews that I conducted during my fieldwork, as well as from the HCAC Internet bulletin board.

CHAPTER 4

1. Hongik Environmental Development Institution, *Hongdae munhwajigu t'adangsŏng chosa* [Feasibility study on the Hongdae cultural district and administration plan] (Seoul: Hongik Environmental Development Institution, 2004), 6.
2. Ibid., 6.
3. Ibid., 98.
4. Ibid., 17.
5. Ibid., 24.
6. Ibid., 192.
7. Ibid., 10.
8. Ibid., 183.
9. Ibid., 17.
10. Ibid.
11. Space Culture Centre, *Space Culture* (Seoul: Space Culture Centre, 2002), 79.
12. Club Culture Association Internet home page, retrieved October 6, 2005 (site discontinued).
13. Muyong Lee, "The Place Marketing Strategy and the Cultural Politics of Space: A Case of the Club Cultures at the Hongdae Area in Seoul" (Ph.D. diss., Seoul National University, 2003) (emphasis in original).
14. City government official, email correspondence with the author, October 5, 2005; Mapo district government official, telephone conversation with the author, March 24, 2006.
15. Lee, interview by the author, Seoul, May 23, 2005.
16. Choi, interview by the author, Seoul, June 9, 2009.
17. Cho, interview by the author, Seoul, March 17, 2006.
18. Cho, interview by the author, Seoul, April 8, 2016.
19. Choi, interview by the author, Seoul, April 16, 2016.
20. Hongdae Culture Academy, "Minutes of the HCA Seminar," February 15, 2006.
21. Ibid.
22. Ibid.
23. Ibid.

24. Ibid.
25. Hongdae Culture Academy, "Minutes of the HCA Seminar," March 7, 2006.
26. Hongdae Culture Academy, "Minutes of the HCA Seminar," February 21, 2006.
27. Ibid.
28. Ibid.
29. Hongdae Culture Academy, "Minutes of the HCA Seminar," March 9, 2006.
30. Hongdae Culture Academy, "Minutes of the HCA Seminar," March 28, 2006.
31. Cho, interview by the author, Seoul, March 27, 2006.
32. Ryu, interview by the author, Seoul, June 9, 2009.
33. Cho, interview by the author, Seoul, May 20, 2009.
34. Choi, interview by the author, Seoul, June 9, 2009.
35. Ibid.
36. Byung Doo Choi, "Shinjayujuŭijŏk Tosihwawa Kiŏpchuŭi Toshi P'ŭrojekt'ŭ" [Neoliberal urbanization and projects of an entrepreneurial city], Han'gukchiyŏkchirihak'oeji [Journal of the Economic Geographical Society of Korea] 14, no. 3 (2011): 263–85. YG Entertainment, one of the largest entertainment companies in Korea, operates as a record label, talent agency, music production company, event management company, and music publisher. Additionally, it runs subsidiary ventures including a franchise restaurant, a clothing line, and a cosmetic brand. It was established in 1996 by one member of the music band Taiji Boys, an iconic band active between 1992 and 1996.
37. Choi, interview by the author, Seoul, April 16, 2016.
38. Hongdae Cultural Studies Network and Seokyo Arts Experiment Center, Hongdaeap munhwayesul saengt'aegye hwalsŏnghwarŭl [A study of the policy for the activation of the culture and art ecosystem in Hongdae area] (Seoul: Seoul Foundation for Arts and Culture, 2014), 4.
39. Juho Chŏng, Chihun Yi, and Chunghan Yoon, "On'lain ŭmak chejaksadŭrŭi chŏllyakchŏk haengdonge kwanhan shilchŭngyŏn'gu" [An empirical study on the strategic behaviors of Korean music producers], Munhwagyŏngjeyŏn'gu [Review of Cultural Economics] 18, no. 2 (2015): 3–20.
40. Jun Michael Park, "Artist Sells Her Trophy during Korean Music Awards," Korea Exposé, March 1 2017, https://www.koreaexpose.com/artist-lee-lang-sells-awards-trophy.
41. Jeha Yi, "Sallong padabi" [Salon Badabie], Street H, February 2012, http://street-h.com/magazine/45170.
42. Thomas Lemke, "'The Birth of Bio-politics': Michel Foucault's Lecture at the Collège de France on Neo-liberal Governmentality," Economy and Society 30, no. 2 (2001): 191.
43. Hongdae Cultural Studies Network and Seokyo Arts Experiment Center, Hongdaeap munhwayesul saengt'aegye hwalsŏnghwarŭl, 40; Kiung Yi, "Chent'ŭrip'ik'eisyŏn hyogwa: Hongdaejiyŏk munhwayuminŭi hŭrŭmgwa taeanjŏk changsoŭi hyŏngsŏng" [Gentrification effects: The flow of cultural refugees and making alternative places in the vicinities of Hongdae], Tosiyŏn'gu [City Studies], no. 14 (2015): 43–85.
44. Hongdae Cultural Studies Network and Seokyo Arts Experiment Center, Hongdaeap munhwayesul saengt'aegye hwalsŏnghwarŭl, 25.
45. Ch'angyŏn Kim, "IMF ihu t'ojishijangbyŏnhwa mit t'ojijŏngch'aek panghyang" [The changes of the land market and the direction of the land policy after the IMF bailout], Chungbuk Report 8, no. 1 (2001): 51–58.

46. Byung Doo Choi, "Tosi jutaegsijang-ŭi byeondongseonggwa budongsan jeongchaeg-ŭi han'gye: IMF wigi ihu seo-ul-eul chungsimŭro" [Volatility of the urban housing market and the limitation of real estate policy: Focused on Seoul and the capital area after the IMF crisis], *Han'gukchiyŏkchirihak'oeji* [Journal of the Economic Geographical Society of Korea] 15, no. 1 (2009): 138–60; Il Paek, "IMF ihu han'gukkyŏngje kujobyŏndonggwa taean: Soyu, saengsan, sobiŭi sahoehwawa munhwasobiŭi chŏllyakchŏk sŭnggyŏk" [Structural change of the Korean economy and its alternatives after the IMF bailout: The socialization of possession, production, and consumption, and the strategic elevation of cultural consumption], *Munhwagwahak* [Cultural Science] 43 (2005): 40–68; Dongŭn Yim and Chongbae Kim, *Met'ŭrop'ollisŭ sŏurŭi t'ansaeng: Sŏurŭi salmŭl mandŭrŏnaen kwŏllyŏk, chabon, chedo kŭrigo yongmangdŭl* [Birth of metropolis Seoul: Power, capital, system that created life in Seoul] (Seoul: Banbi, 2015); Sang-u Yun, "IMF wigi ihu shinjayujuŭiŭi naebuhwa kwajŏng: Han'gukkwa pŭrajil pigyo" [A comparative study on internalization of neoliberalism in Korea and Brazil], *Asea yŏn'gu* [Journal of Asiatic Studies] 56, no. 3 (2013): 364–95.

47. Kim, "IMF ihu t'ojishijangbyŏnhwa mit t'ojijŏngch'aek panghyang."

48. Choi, "Tosi jutaegsijang-ŭi byeondongseonggwa budongsan jeongchaeg-ŭi han'gye," 145–46.

49. Minho Kuk, "Kukkajudoesŏ kiŏpchudoro: IMF oehwanwigi ihu kukkawa chaebŏlgwaŭi kwan'gye pyŏnhwa" [From state-led to chaebol-led: The changing relationship between the state and chaebols after the IMF foreign exchange crisis], *Hyŏnsanggwa Inshik* [Korean Journal of Humanities and the Social Sciences] 35, no. 3 (2011): 129–58.

50. Yun, "IMF wigi ihu shinjayujuŭiŭi naebuhwa kwajŏng."

51. Choi, "Tosi jutaegsijang-ŭi byeondongseonggwa budongsan jeongchaeg-ŭi han'gye."

52. Peter Moskowitz, *How to Kill a City: Gentrification, Inequality, and the Fight for the Neighborhood* (New York: Nation Books, 2017), 9.

53. Jean-Pierre Olivier de Sardan, *Anthropology and Development: Understanding Contemporary Social Change*, trans. Antoinette Tidjani Alou (London: Zed Books, 2005); Marion Fourcade, *Economists and Societies: Discipline and Profession in the United States, Britain, and France, 1890s to 1990s* (Princeton, NJ: Princeton University Press, 2009).

CHAPTER 5

1. Ray Oldenburg, *The Great Good Place: Cafés, Coffee Shops, Bookstores, Bars, Hair Salons, and Other Hangouts at the Heart of a Community* (New York: Marlowe, 1999).

2. Peter Moskowitz, *How to Kill a City: Gentrification, Inequality, and the Fight for the Neighborhood* (New York: Nation Books, 2017), 9.

3. Ibid.

4. Sooah Kim, "Hongdae konggan ŭi Munhwajŏk ŭimi pyŏnhwa: Konggan iyongjaŭi kiŏkŭl chungsimŭro" [Changes in the cultural meaning of the Hongdae place: Focused on the memories of place users], *Midiŏ, Chendŏ wa Munhwa* [Media, Gender, and Culture] 30, no. 4 (2015): 83–123.

5. Quoted in Minha Pak, "Naesaengjŏk yoinŭi toshimunhwak'ont'ench'ŭhwae kwanhan chŏkyongganŭngsŏng yŏn'gu: Hongdae chiyŏkŭl chungshimŭro" [A study on the application validity of the endogenous factor to subculture contents: In the case of Hongik University area], *Munhwak'ŏnt'ench'ŭ Yŏgu* [Journal of Cultural Contents], no. 2 (2012): 158.

6. Korea Performance Art Spirit, "Kimbaekki yesulgamdok, kŭrŭl algo shipta: 2016 chejugukcheshirhŏmyesulche kimbaekki yesulgamdokkwaŭi taehwa" [Kim Baek Gi, artistic director, we want to know him: Conversations with director Kim at the 2016 Jeju International Experimental Arts Festival], *Story Funding*, September 9, 2016, https://storyfunding.daum.net/episode/11724.

7. Kihong Yu, *Hongdaeap indiŭmang saengt'aegyeŭi wigiwa taean* [The crisis of the ecology of Hongdae indie music and its solution] (Seoul: National Assembly Research Service, 2015).

8. Hongdae Cultural Studies Network and Seokyo Arts Experiment Center, *Hongdaeap munhwayesul saengt'aegye hwalsŏnghwarŭl wihan chŏngch'aekyŏn'gugwaje* [A study of the policy for the activation of the culture and art ecosystem in Hongdae area] (Seoul: Seoul Foundation for Arts and Culture, 2014); Sooah Kim, *Sŏulshi munhwagongganŭi tamnonjŏk kusŏng: Hongdae kongganŭl chungshimŭro* [Discursive structure of the cultural space in Seoul: Focused on Hongdae area] (Seoul: Seoul Institute, 2013); Kiung Yi, "Chent'ŭrip'ik'eisyŏn hyogwa: Hongdaejiyŏk munhwayuminŭi hŭrŭmgwa taeanjŏk changsoŭi hyŏngsŏng" [Gentrification effects: The flow of cultural refugees and making alternative places in the vicinities of Hongdae], *Tosiyŏn'gu* [City Studies], no. 14 (2015): 43–85.

9. Yi, "Chent'ŭrip'ik'eisyŏn hyogwa," 66.

10. Jung, interview by the author, Seoul, April 14, 2016.

11. Jiyŏn Chŏng, "Ŏtchŏdat't . . . kage" [Accidentally . . . store], *Street H*, April 2014, http://street-h.com/magazine/74216.

12. Cho, interview by the author, Seoul, April 8, 2016.

13. Ibid.

14. Ibid.

15. Ibid.

16. David Harvey, *A Brief History of Neoliberalism* (Oxford: Oxford University Press, 2007).

17. Luc Boltaniski, "The Left after May 1968 and the Longing for Total Revolution," *Thesis Eleven* 69, no. 1 (2002): 1–20.

18. Ibid.

19. Luc Boltanski and Ève Chiapello, *The New Spirit of Capitalism*, trans. Gregory Elliott (New York: Verso, 2007).

20. Yoshiyuki Sato, *Shin jiyushuhi to kenryoku* [Neoliberalism and power], trans. Kim Sangwun (Seoul: Humanitas, 2014), 50, 51.

21. Jung, interview by the author.

22. Seoul Social Economy Portal, "Sogae: Sahoejŏkkyŏngje" [Introduction: Social economy], http://sehub.net/policy (accessed October 14, 2017).

23. Jung, interview by the author.

24. Ibid.

25. Ibid.

26. Zygmunt Bauman, *Work, Consumerism and the New Poor* (Berkshire, UK: McGraw-Hill, 2004).

27. Jung, interview by the author.

28. David Throsby, *The Economics of Cultural Policy* (Cambridge: Cambridge University Press, 2010), 21.

29. Daniel Miller, "The Uses of Value," *Geoforum* 39, no. 3 (2008): 1123.

30. Choi, interview by the author, Seoul, April 16, 2016.

31. Ibid.

32. Ibid.

33. Ibid.

34. Ibid.

35. Ibid.

36. Ibid.

37. Ibid.

38. Sung, interview by the author, Seoul, April 13, 2016.

39. Ibid.

40. Ibid.

41. Ibid.

42. Ibid.

43. Ibid.

44. Herbert Marcuse, *One-Dimensional Man: Studies in the Ideology of Advanced Industrial Society*, 2nd ed. (London: Routledge, 2013).

45. Sung, interview by the author.

46. Ibid.

47. Ibid.

48. Cha, interview by the author, Seoul, April 10, 2016.

49. Ibid.

50. Ibid.

51. Boltanski and Chiapello, *The New Spirit of Capitalism*, 38.

52. Ibid.

53. Joseph Heath and Andrew Potter, *Nation of Rebels: Why Counterculture Became Consumer Culture* (New York: HarperCollins, 2004).

CONCLUSION

1. Jinsong Kim, *Sŏure ttansŭhorŭl hŏhara* [Allow dance halls in Seoul] (Seoul: Hyŏnshilmunhwayŏn'gu, 1999). The article was originally featured in the January 1937 issue of *Samchoenri*.

2. Kim, *Sŏure ttansŭhorŭl hŏhara*, 65–66.

3. Ibid., 66.

4. William H. Sewell, Jr., "A Theory of Structure: Duality, Agency, and Transformation," *American Journal of Sociology* 98, no. 1 (1992): 29.

5. Ibid.

6. Max Weber, *The Protestant Ethic and the Spirit of Capitalism*, trans. Stephen Kalberg (London: Routledge, 2010).

7. Daniel Cohen, *Three Lectures on Post-Industrial Society* (Cambridge, MA: MIT Press, 2009), 22.

8. Ibid.

9. Ibid., 25.

10. Luc Boltanski and Ève Chiapello, *The New Spirit of Capitalism*, trans. Gregory Elliott (New York: Verso, 2007); Cohen, *Three Lectures on Post-industrial Society*.

11. Jesook Song, *South Koreans in the Debt Crisis: The Creation of a Neoliberal Welfare Society* (Durham, NC: Duke University Press, 2009).

12. Kyung-Sup Chang, "Economic Development, Democracy and Citizenship Politics in South Korea: The Predicament of Developmental Citizenship," *Citizenship Studies* 16, no. 1 (2012): 29–47.

13. Zygmunt Bauman, *Liquid Times: Living in an Age of Uncertainty* (Cambridge, UK: Polity, 2011).

14. Hannah Arendt, *The Human Condition*, 2nd ed. (Chicago, IL: University of Chicago Press, 2013).

15. Bauman, *Liquid Times*, 110.

16. Flyer with Mapo district's guide to the Hongdae area, 2015; Hongik Environmental Development Institution, *Hongdae munhwajigu t'adangsŏng chosa mit kwalligyehoek suribyŏngua* [Feasibility study on the Hongdae cultural district and on the administration plan] (Seoul: Hongik Environmental Development Institution, 2004).

Bibliography

Arendt, Hannah. *The Human Condition.* 2nd ed. Chicago: University of Chicago Press, 2013.

Associated News. "Hongdae shinch'on tŭng munhwajigu chijŏngdoenda" [Hongdae and Shinchon will be demarcated as cultural districts]. *Hankoyreh 21* (Seoul), September 18, 2003. http://legacy.www.hani.co.kr/section-005000000/2003/09/005000000020 0309181322001.html.

Barnes, Trevor, and Thomas A. Hutton. "Situating the New Economy: Contingencies of Regeneration and Dislocation in Vancouver's Inner City." *Urban Studies* 46, no. 5–6 (2009): 1247–69.

Bauman, Zygmunt. *Liquid Times: Living in an Age of Uncertainty.* Cambridge, UK: Polity, 2011.

Bauman, Zygmunt. *Work, Consumerism and the New Poor.* Berkshire, UK: McGraw-Hill, 2004.

Bell, David, and Mark Jayne, eds. *City of Quarters: Urban Villages in the Contemporary City.* Aldershot, UK: Ashgate, 2004.

Berman, Marshall. *All That Is Solid Melts into Air: The Experience of Modernity.* New York: Verso, 1983.

Bianchini, Franco. "Cultural Planning in Post-industrial Societies." In *Cultural Planning: Center for Urbanism,* edited by Katrine Østergaard, 13–24. Copenhagen: Royal Danish Academy of Fine Arts, 2004.

Bianchini, Franco, and Lia Ghilardi. "The Culture of Neighbourhoods: A European Perspective." In *City of Quarters: Urban Villages in the Contemporary City,* edited by David Bell and Mark Jayne, 237–48. Aldershot, UK: Ashgate, 2004.

Bierschenk, Thomas, and Jean-Pierre Olivier de Sardan. "ECRIS: Rapid Collective Inquiry for the Identification of Conflicts and Strategic Groups." *Human Organization* 56, no. 2 (1997): 238–44.

Blue Ribbon Survey. *Hongdae matchip 427* [Delicious restaurants in Hongdae area 427]. Seoul: BRmedia, 2016.

Boltanski, Luc. "The Left after May 1968 and the Longing for Total Revolution." *Thesis Eleven* 69, no. 1 (2002): 1–20.

Boltanski, Luc, and Ève Chiapello. "The New Spirit of Capitalism." Paper presented at the Conference of Europeanists, Chicago, March 14–16, 2002.

Boltanski, Luc, and Ève Chiapello. *The New Spirit of Capitalism.* Translated by Gregory Elliott. New York: Verso, 2007.

Campbell, John L. "Ideas, Politics, and Public Policy." *Annual Review of Sociology* 28, no. 1 (2002): 21–38.

Ch'a, U-jin. "Toshi gyehoek kwa hongdae-ap indissin: Wae 1996 nyŏnin'ga?" [Urban planning and indie scene of Hongdae area: Why 1996?]. *P'ŭllaetp'om* [Platform], no. 45 (2014): 68–73.

Chang, Kyung-Sup. "Economic Development, Democracy and Citizenship Politics in South Korea: The Predicament of Developmental Citizenship." *Citizenship Studies* 16, no. 1 (2012): 29–47.

Cho, Ara. "Sŏulshi kesŭt'ŭhausŭ Hongdaeap 158 kot, 1 wi" [Hongdae area guesthouse 158, top of Seoul]. *Street H*, March 2015. http://street-h.com/magazine/89037.

Cho, Gabi. "Pinbŭradŏsŭ: K'ŏp'iŭi Aput'ŏ Zkkaji mannal su innŭn kot pinbŭradŏsŭ" [Bean Brothers: Factory-type café where you can taste the A to Z of coffee]. *Street H*, August 2014. http://street-h.com/magazine/81041.

Cho, Hŭiyŏn. "Hegemoni kusŏngjŏk kwajŏnggwa 'hegemoni kyunyŏlt': Kukmin, minjung, shiminŭi tonghak" [The process of constructing hegemony and the "fissure of hegemony": Dynamics of nation, people, and citizen]. In *Tongwŏndoen kŭndaehwa: Pak Chŏng-hŭi kaebal tongwŏn ch'eje ŭi chŏngch'i sahoejŏk ijungsŏng* [Mobilized modernization: The political and social duality under Park Jung Hee's developmental mobilization regime], 331–77. Seoul: Humanitas, 2010.

Cho, Mihye. "Mapping the Hong-Dae Area in Seoul: A New and Unstable Economic Space?" In *New Economic Spaces in Asian Cities: From Industrial Restructuring to the Cultural Turn*, edited by Peter W. Daniels, K. C. Ho, and Thomas A. Hutton, 133–49. London: Routledge, 2012.

Cho, Myung-Rae. "Flexible Sociality and the Postmodernity of Seoul." *Korea Journal* 39, no. 3 (1999): 122–42.

Choi, Byung Doo. "Shinjayujuŭijŏk toshihwawa kiŏpchuŭi toshi p'ŭrojekt'ŭ" [Neoliberal urbanization and projects of an entrepreneurial city]. *Han'gukchiyŏkchirihak'oeji* [Journal of the Economic Geographical Society of Korea] 14, no. 3 (2011): 263–85.

Choi, Byung Doo. "Tosi jutaegsijang-ŭi byeondongseonggwa budongsan jeongchaeg-ŭi han'gye: IMF wigi ihu seo-ul-eul chungsimŭro" [Volatility of the urban housing market and the limitation of real estate policy: Focused on Seoul and the capital area after the IMF crisis]. *Han'gukchiyŏkchirihak'oeji* [Journal of the Economic Geographical Society of Korea] 15, no. 1 (2009): 138–60.

Choi, Hyŏn. "Shijangin'ganŭi hyŏngsŏng: Saenghwalsegyeŭi shingminhwawa chŏhang" [Birth of a market person: Colonization and resistance of the lifeworld]. *Tonghyang-gwa Chŏnmang* [Trend and Prospect] 81 (February 2011): 156–94.

Choi, Sŏhŭi. "Hongdaeap munhwa chik'igi" [Protecting Hongdae culture]. *KBS News* (Seoul), February 11, 2004. http://news.kbs.co.kr/news/view.do?ncd=541059.

Choi, Yŏnghwa. "Yi myŏngngbak chŏngbuŭi kiŏpkukka p'ŭrojekt'ŭrosŏ hallyujŏngch'aek: Chŏllyakkwan'gyejŏk chŏpkŭnbŏbŭl t'onghan kujowa chŏllyak punsŏk" [The Korean-wave policy as a corporate-state project of the Lee government: The analysis of structures and strategies based on the strategic-relational approach]. *Kyŏngjewa Sahoe* [Economy and Society], no. 97 (2013): 252–85.

Chŏn, Wŏn'gyŏng. "Han'guk tŭrama such'ul huwŏnjŏngch'aegŭi hyoyulsŏnge taehan koch'al: 1995–2005 rŭl chungshimŭro" [A study of the efficiencies of Korean drama export support policies: Between 1995 and 2005]. *Küllobŏlmunhwak'ont'ench'ŭ* [Global Cultural Content], no. 14 (2014): 153–78.

Chŏng, Gabyŏng. "Urinara munhwajŏngch'aegŭi inyŏme kwanhan yŏn'gu" [A study on cultural political ideas in South Korea]. *Munhwajŏngch'aengnonch'ong* [Journal of Cultural Policy] 5 (December 1993): 82–132.

Chŏng, Gwanung. "Yojŭm chŏlmŭn X-sedaeŭi tŭngjanggwa t'ŭkching" [The emergence and the characteristics of Generation X]. *MBC News* (Seoul), April 5, 1994. http://imnews.imbc.com/20dbnews/history/1994/1926247_19434.html.

Chŏng, Jiyŏn. "Khapheyka chwuek sokulo kelewassta: Pihaintu censi" [Café strolling down memory lane: Behind exhibition]. *Street H*, April 2013. http://street-h.com/magazine/45387.

Chŏng, Jiyŏn. "Ŏtchŏdat't . . . kage" [Accidentally . . . a store]. *Street H*, April 2014. http://street-h.com/magazine/74216.

Chŏng, Jiyŏn. "'Paul Avril': Kŭdŭrŭi konggani kunggŭmhada" [Paul Avril: Curious about their spaces], *Street H*, June 2013. http://street-h.com/magazine/45237.

Chŏng, Jongŭn. "Han'guk munhwajŏngch'aegŭi ch'angjojŏk chŏnhoe: Chayu, t'uja, ch'angjosŏng" [The creative turn of Korean cultural policy: Freedom, investment, and creativity]. *In'ganyŏn'gu* [Human Studies], no. 25 (2013): 33–71.

Chŏng, Juho, Chihun Yi, and Chunghan Yoon. "On'lain ŭmak chejaksadŭrŭi chŏllyakchŏk haengdonge kwanhan shilchŭngyŏn'gu" [An empirical study on the strategic behaviors of Korean music producers]. *Munhwagyŏngjeyŏn'gu* [Review of Cultural Economics] 18, no. 2 (2015): 3–20.

Club Culture Association. *K'ŭllŏmmunhwa* [Club culture]. Seoul: Club Culture Association, 2004.

Cohen, Daniel. *Three Lectures on Post-industrial Society*. Cambridge, MA: MIT Press, 2009.

Florida, Richard. *The Rise of the Creative Class: And How It's Transforming Work, Leisure, Community and Everyday Life*. New York: Basic Books, 2002.

Fourcade, Marion. *Economists and Societies: Discipline and Profession in the United States, Britain, and France, 1890s to 1990s*. Princeton, NJ: Princeton University Press, 2009.

Fourcade-Gourinchas, Marion, and Sarah L. Babb. "The Rebirth of the Liberal Creed: Paths to Neoliberalism in Four Countries." *American Journal of Sociology* 108, no. 3 (2002): 533–79.

Fuller, Crispian. "'Worlds of Justification' in the Politics and Practices of Urban Regeneration." *Environment and Planning D: Society and Space* 30, no. 5 (2012): 913–29.

Gang, Sinae. "Chaseytay noli kongkan 'Pokhapmwunhwakhaphey'" [Next generation play space, "multicultural café"], *Goodtimezine*, April 2006.

Ghilardi, Lia. "Cultural Planning and Cultural Diversity." In *Differing Diversities: Transversal Study on the Theme of Cultural Policy and Cultural Diversity*, edited by Tony Bennett, 116–27. Strasbourg, France: Council of Europe, 2001.

Giddens, Anthony. *Capitalism and Modern Social Theory: An Analysis of the Writings of Marx, Durkheim and Max Weber*. Cambridge: Cambridge University Press, 2011.

Gornostacva, Galina, and Noel Campbell. "The Creative Underclass in the Production of Place: Example of Camden Town in London." *Journal of Urban Affairs* 34, no. 2 (2012): 169–88.

"Hallyu (Korean Wave)." *Korea.net*. http://www.korea.net/AboutKorea/Culture-and-the-Arts/Hallyu (accessed August 24, 2018).

Han, Yŏngju, Muyong Lee, Jaehyŏn Yu, Ram Hae, and Todorok'i Hirosi. *Wŏltŭkŏp chŏllyakchiyŏk changsomak'et'ing: Hongdaejiyŏk munhwahwalsŏnghwa pangan* [Place marketing of the (2002) World Cup strategic areas: Schemes for vitalizing culture in Hongdae]. Seoul: Seoul Development Institute, 2000.

Han'gukshirhŏmyesulchŏngshin [Korea Performance Art Spirit]. *Segye shirhŏmyesurŭi mek'a hongdaeap* [Mecca of experimental art in the world, Hongdae area]. Seoul: Symposium, 2009.

Harvey, David. *A Brief History of Neoliberalism*. Oxford: Oxford University Press, 2007.

Harvey, David. *The Condition of Postmodernity: An Enquiry into the Origins of Cultural Change*. Oxford: Blackwell, 1989.

Heath, Joseph, and Andrew Potter. *Nation of Rebels: Why Counterculture Became Consumer Culture*. New York: HarperCollins, 2004.

Hesmondhalgh, David, and Andy C. Pratt. "Cultural Industries and Cultural Policy." *International Journal of Cultural Policy* 11, no. 1 (2005): 1–13.

Hongdae Cultural Studies Network and Seokyo Arts Experiment Center. *Hongdaeap munhwayesul saengt'aegye hwalsŏnghwarŭl wihan chŏngch'aekyŏn'gugwaje* [A study of the policy for the activation of the culture and art ecosystem in Hongdae area]. Seoul: Seoul Foundation for Arts and Culture, 2014.

Hongdae Culture Academy. "Minutes of the HCA Seminar." February 15, 2006.

Hongdae Culture Academy. "Minutes of the HCA Seminar." February 21, 2006.

Hongdae Culture Academy. "Minutes of the HCA Seminar." March 7, 2006.

Hongdae Culture Academy. "Minutes of the HCA Seminar." March 9, 2006.

Hongdae Culture Academy. "Minutes of the HCA Seminar." March 28, 2006.

Hongdae Culture and Arts Cooperation. Flyer distributed during the opening ceremony of the HCAC. February 19, 2004.

Hongdae Culture and Arts Cooperation. "Minutes of the HCAC." January 20, 2004.

Hongdae Culture and Arts Cooperation. "Minutes of the HCAC." January 28, 2004.

Hongdae Culture and Arts Cooperation. "Minutes of the Meeting for the Establishment of the HCAC." January 20, 2004.

Hongik Environmental Development Institution. *Hongdae munhwajigu t'adangsŏng chosa mit kwalligyehoek suribyŏn'gua* [Feasibility study on the Hongdae cultural district and administration plan]. Seoul: Hongik Environmental Development Institution, 2004.

"Hot Nights at Hongdae's Hottest Clubs." *VisitSeoul.net*, January 3, 2016. http://english .visitseoul.net/tours/Hot-Nights-at-Hongdae's-HottestClubs_/579.

Hutton, Thomas A. *The New Economy of the Inner City: Restructuring, Regeneration and Dislocation in the Twenty-First Century Metropolis*. New York: Routledge, 2009.

Inmunk'ont'ench'ŭhak'oe [Human Contents Academy]. *Munhwak'ont'ench'ŭ immun* [Introduction to cultural contents]. Seoul: Bookkorea, 2006.

Jongno District Office. "Daehakro munhwajigu kwalligyehoek" [Administrative plan of Daehakro cultural district]. 2005. http://www.sfac.or.kr/artbattery/images/down load/%EC%9E%AC%EB%8B%A8%20%EA%B5%AD%EB%AC%B8%20%EB%B8 %8C%EB%A1%9C%EC%8A%88%EC%96%B4%202014.pdf.

Kim, Aejin. *Chigŭmŭn Hongdae sŭt'ail: 101 kaji chŭlgŏumi kadŭk'an kot* [Now Hongdae style: 101 places full of joy]. Seoul: Ungjinthinkbig, 2012.

Kim, Ch'angyŏn. "IMF ihu t'ojishijangbyŏnhwa mit t'ojijŏngch'aek panghyang" [The changes of the land market and the direction of the land policy after the IMF bailout]. *Chungbuk Report* 8, no. 1 (2001): 51–58.

Kim, Chŏngsu. "Yech'ŭkpulga'ŭi mihak: Hallyuesŏ paeunŭn munhwajŏngch'aegŭi kyohun" [The beauty of the unpredictability: Cultural policy lessons of the Korean wave]. Paper presented at the Seoul Association for Public Administration International Conference, Seoul, October 27, 2006.

Kim, Gogŭm. "Hongdaeap k'ŭllŏp, puhwarinya, mollaginya: 'Pulp'yŏngdŭng kong-yŏnbŏbŭro kosa wigi' chiptan panbal" [Hongdae clubs, revival or collapse: Group resistance of the crisis of the decline by "unequal performance act"]. *Munhwa Daily* (Seoul), July 22, 2006. http://www.munhwa.com/news/view.html?no=20060722 010301300730024.

Kim, Jakka. "'K'auntŏ k'ŏlch'ŏ' ka sarajin hongdaeap" [Hongdae area, where "counter culture" disappeared]. *Kyunghyang Shinmun* [Kyunghyang Daily News] (Seoul), September 30, 2014. http://news.khan.co.kr/kh_news/khan_art_view.html?code= 990100&artid=201409302130075.

Kim, Jakka. "Why: Hongdaeap indibaendeuui sijag-eun . . ." [Why: The beginning of Hongdae indie bands . . .]. *Chosun Shinmun* [Chosun Daily News] (Seoul), March 14, 2008. http://newsplus.chosun.com/site/data/html_dir/2010/03/11/2010031101867 .html.

Kim, Jinae. "Sŏul hongdaeap: Koetchadŭrŭi 'yesulch'anggo' . . . 'indi chŏngshin' hwal shiwirŭl tanggyŏra" [Hongdae area in Seoul: "Art storage" of loonies . . . "Indie spirit" pulls the Bowstring]. *Chosun Shinmun* [Chosun Daily News] (Seoul), February 25, 2002.

Kim, Jinsong. *Sŏure ttansŭhorŭl hŏhara* [Allow dance halls in Seoul]. Seoul: Hyŏn-shilmunhwayŏn'gu, 1999.

Kim, Jisoo, *K'ŭllik! Taejungmunhwa-ga poyŏyo* [Click! Mass culture is seen]. Seoul: Munhwamadang, 1999.

Kim, Jonghwi. Preface to *Narara baendeu ttwieora indi* [Fly bands, run indie], edited by An Iyŏngno, Kim Jonhwi, Mun Sŏk, Shin Hyunjoon, and Sung Gi-Wan, 4–25. Seoul: Hanaem, 2000.

Kim, Jongyun. "Hongdaeap'e shinsedae p'aesyŏnhaeng" [New generation fashion street in Hongdae area]. *JoongAng Daily* (Seoul), April 21, 1995. http://news.joins.com/ article/3051860.

Kim, Jun. "Sŏul hongdaeap munhwajigu chijŏng" [Hongdae area is demarcated as cultural district]. *Kyunghyang Shinmun* [Kyunghyang Daily News] (Seoul), January 11, 2003. http://news.khan.co.kr/kh_news/khan_art_view.html?code=950201&artid= 20030110055101.

Kim, Min'gyŏng. "Hongdae wŏnjumindŭrŭi moim 'honghap': Hongdaemunhwa salligo saengjon'gwŏn chik'igo" [Gathering of Hongdae natives "Honghap": Save Hongdae culture and the right to live]. *Weekly Donga* (Seoul), February 20, 2004. http:// weekly.donga.com/List/3/all/11/73125/1.

Kim, Pyŏla. "Chŏngch'unsongga, kŭdŭri taeshin ulmyŏ purŭda" [An ode to youth, they cried out for us]. In *K'ŭraing nŏt: Kŭdŭri taeshin ulbujitta* [Crying Nut: They cried out for us], edited by Sŭngho Chi, 183–235. Seoul: Outsider, 2002.

Kim, Sooah. "Hongdae konggan ŭi munhwajŏk ŭimi pyŏnhwa: Konggan iyongjaŭi kiŏkŭl chungsimŭro" [Changes in the cultural meaning of the Hongdae place: Focused on the memories of place users]. *Midiŏ, Chendŏ wa Munhwa* [Media, Gender, and Culture] 30, no. 4 (2015): 83–123.

Kim, Sooah. *Sŏulshi munhwagongganŭi tamnonjŏk kusŏng: Hongdae konggganŭl chungshimŭro* [Discursive structure of the cultural space in Seoul: Focused on Hongdae area]. Seoul: Seoul Institute, 2013.

Kim, Yŏnchin. "Munhwajiguŭi munjejŏmgwa kaesŏn panghyang" [Problems of and improvements for the cultural district]. *Hwan'gyŏngnonch'ong* [Journal of Environmental Studies] 51 (December 2012): 115–29.

Kim, Yunjong. "Hongdaeap = indimunhwa mek'a t'oesaek" [Tarnishing Hongdae area = indie mecca]. *Donga Daily* (Seoul), August 6, 2005. http://news.donga.com/3/all/20050806/8216791/1.

Klein, Naomi. *No Logo: Taking Aim at the Brand Bullies*. New York: Picador, 2000.

Korea Culture Policy Institute. *Munhwajigu chosŏng modelgaebal mit chŏngch'aekpanghyange kwanhan yŏn'gu* [Research on cultural district development and policy direction]. Seoul: Korea Culture Policy Institute, 1999.

Korea Culture Policy Institute. *Munhwajŏngch'esŏng hwangnibŭl wihan chŏngch'aekpangan yŏn'gu* [A study on the policy measures for establishing cultural identity]. Seoul: Korea Culture Policy Institute, 2002.

Korea Culture Policy Institute. *Munhwatosi mit munhwabelt'ŭ chosŏngbangan yŏn'gu* [A study on designation and development of the cultural city or cultural belt]. Seoul: Korea Culture Policy Institute, 2000.

Korea Performance Art Spirit. "Kimbaekki yesulgamdok, kŭrŭl algo shipta: 2016 chejugukcheshirhŏmyesulche kimbaekki yesulgamdokkwaŭi taehwa" [Kim Baek Gi, artistic director, we want to know him: Conversations with director Kim at the 2016 Jeju International Experimental Arts Festival]. *Story Funding*, September 9, 2016. https://storyfunding.daum.net/episode/11724.

Korea Tourism Organization. *2010 munhwagangguk (C-Korea 2010) yuksŏngjŏllyak* [Strategy for C-Korea 2010]. Seoul: Korea Tourism Organization, 2005.

Kuk, Minho. "Kukkajudoesŏ kiŏpchudoro: IMF oehwanwigi ihu kukkawa chaebŏlgwaŭi kwan'gye pyŏnhwa" [From state-led to chaebol-led: The changing relationship between the state and chaebols after the IMF foreign exchange crisis]. *Hyŏnsanggwa Inshik* [Korean Journal of Humanities and the Social Sciences] 35, no. 3 (2011): 129–58.

"K'ŭllŏptei chungdanŭl t'onghae hongdaeapkwa k'ŭllŏbŭl yaegihada" [Speaking on Hongdae and Hongdae clubs through the discontinuation of Club Day]. *Street H*, February 2011. http://street-h.com/magazine/44979.

Kwŏn, Ch'angkyu. "Munhwa'esŏ t'rk'ont'ench'ŭ'ro: Han'guk munhwaŭi sanŏp'wawa hallyuhwarŭl chungshimŭro" [The transition from culture to contents: Focusing on the industrialization of Korean culture and the Korean wave]. *Taejungsŏsayŏn'gu* [Journal of Popular Narrative] 20, no. 3 (2014): 221–44.

Kwon, Huck-Ju. "Advocacy Coalitions and the Politics of Welfare in Korea after the Economic Crisis." *Policy and Politics* 31, no. 1 (2003): 69–83.

Landry, Charles. *The Creative City: A Toolkit for Urban Innovators*. 2nd ed. London: Earthscan, 2009.

Lash, Scott, and John Urry. *Economies of Signs and Space*. London: Sage, 1994.

Lee, Muyong. "The Landscape of Club Culture and Identity Politics: Focusing on the Club Culture in the Hongdae Area of Seoul." *Korea Journal* 44, no. 3 (2004): 65–107.

Lee, Muyong. "The Place Marketing Strategy and the Cultural Politics of Space: A Case of the Club Cultures at the Hongdae Area in Seoul." Ph.D. diss., Seoul National University, 2003.

Lemke, Thomas. "'The Birth of Bio-politics': Michel Foucault's Lecture at the Collège de France on Neo-liberal Governmentality." *Economy and Society* 30, no. 2 (2001): 190–207.

Long, Norman. "Exploring Local/Global Transformations: A View from Anthropology." In *Anthropology, Development and Modernities: Exploring Discourses, Counter-tendencies and Violence*, edited by Alberto Arce and Norman Long, 184–201. London: Routledge, 2000.

MacCannell, Dean. *The Tourist: A New Theory of the Leisure Class*. Rev. ed. Berkeley: University of California Press, 1989.

Mapo desainch'ulp'anchinhŭngjiguhyŏbŭihoe [Mapo Design and Publication Promotion Association]. *Hongdaeap tijaint'pch'ulp'an chido* [Design and publication map of Hongdae area]. Seoul: Propaganda, 2015.

Mapo District Office. *Hangout in Hongdae*. Seoul: Mapo District Office, 2013.

Mapo District Office. *Hongdaeap ch'omch'om kaidŭ: Hongdaeap soksoktŭri chŭlgigi* [Hongdae area guide: Enjoy everything in the Hongdae area]. Seoul: Mapo District Office, 2010.

Mapo District Office. "Households and Population by Dong (Resident Registration)." 2017. http://www.mapo.go.kr/CmsWeb/resource/image/stat2013/pdf/year 2017/3.pdf.

Mapo District Office. *Mapo District's Guide to the Hongdae Area*. Seoul: Mapo District Office, 2015.

Marcuse, Herbert. *One-Dimensional Man: Studies in the Ideology of Advanced Industrial Society*. 2nd ed. London: Routledge, 2013.

Maŭryŏndae [Community Union]. *Irŏn maŭresŏ salgoshipta, 2002: Maŭlmandŭlgi paeksŏ* [Want to live in this community, 2002: Community-making white paper]. Seoul: Maŭryŏndae, 2003.

McGuigan, Jim. *Cool Capitalism*. London: Pluto, 2009.

McGuigan, Jim. *Culture and the Public Sphere*. London: Routledge, 1996.

Miller, Daniel. "The Uses of Value." *Geoforum* 39, no. 3 (2008): 1122–32.

Ministry of Culture and Sports. *2014 munhwajŏngch'aekpaeksŏ* [2014 cultural policy white paper]. Seoul: Ministry of Culture and Sports, 2015.

Ministry of Culture and Tourism. *Munhwagangguk (C-Korea) 2010: Munhwaro punganghago haengbok'an taehanmin'gugŭi miraejŏllyak* [The cultural power (C-Korea) 2010: The future strategies for wealthy and happy Korea through culture]. Seoul: Ministry of Culture and Sports, 2005.

Ministry of Culture and Tourism. *2002 munhwajŏngch'aekpaeksŏ* [2002 cultural policy white paper]. Seoul: Ministry of Culture and Sports, 2003.

Ministry of Culture and Tourism. *2009 munhwajŏngch'aekpaeksŏ* [2009 cultural policy white paper]. Seoul: Ministry of Culture and Sports, 2010.

Mommaas, Hans. "Cultural Clusters and the Post-industrial City: Towards the Remapping of Urban Cultural Policy." *Urban Studies* 41, no. 3 (2004): 507–32.

Moskowitz, Peter. *How to Kill a City: Gentrification, Inequality, and the Fight for the Neighborhood*. New York: Nation Books, 2017.

Nam, Hojin. "Pul kkŏjyŏganŭn sŏul hongdaeap raibŭk'ŭllŏp" [Dimming Hongdae live clubs in Seoul]. *Kyunghyang Shinmun* [Kyunghyang Daily News] (Seoul), November 19, 2006. http://news.khan.co.kr/kh_news/khan_art_view.html?code=210000&artid=200611191650271.

O, Yangyŏl. "Han'gugŭi munhwahaengjŏngch'egye 50 nyŏn: Kujo mit kinŭngŭi pyŏnch'ŏn'gwajŏnggwa kŭ kwaje" [Fifty years of the cultural administration systems in South Korea: The process of transition and its task of structure and function].

Munhwajŏngch'aengnonch'ong [Journal of Cultural Policy] 7 (December 1995): 29–74.

Oldenburg, Ray. *The Great Good Place: Cafés, Coffee Shops, Bookstores, Bars, Hair Salons, and Other Hangouts at the Heart of a Community.* New York: Marlowe, 1999.

Olivier de Sardan, Jean-Pierre. *Anthropology and Development: Understanding Contemporary Social Change.* Translated by Antoinette Tidjani Alou. London: Zed Books, 2005.

Paek, Il. "IMF ihu han'gukkyŏngje kujobyŏndonggwa taean: Soyu, saengsan, sobiŭi sahoehwawa munhwasobiŭi chŏllyakchŏk sŭnggyŏk" [Structural change of the Korean economy and its alternatives after the IMF bailout: The socialization of possession, production, and consumption, and the strategic elevation of cultural consumption]. *Munhwagwahak* [Cultural Science] 43 (September 2005): 40–68.

Pak, Hyemin. "Kam chabatta, t'rnŭkkimp'yot' k'aejuŏl" [Sensed it, "!" casual]. *JoongAng Daily* (Seoul), November 8, 2002. http://news.joins.com/article/4375241.

Pak, Minha. "Naesaengjŏk yoinŭi toshimunhwak'ont'ench'ŭhwae kwanhan chŏkyongganŭngsŏng yŏn'gu: Hongdae chiyŏkŭl chungshimŭro" [A study on the application validity of the endogenous factor to subculture contents: In the case of Hongik University area]. *Munhwak'ont'ench'ŭ Yŏn'gu* [Journal of Cultural Contents], no. 2 (2012): 125–66.

Pak, Suryŏn, and Haeyong Son. "'Hongdaeap munhwa' ka tansok taesang?" [Is "Hongdae culture" a target of crackdown?]. *JoongAng Daily* (Seoul), August 3, 2005. http://news.joins.com/article/1649587.

Pak, Young-Jeong. "Historical Distinctiveness of Korean Cultural Policy: Present and Future." Paper presented at the 2016 International Conference on Cultural Policy Research, Seoul, July 6, 2016.

Park, Jun Michael. "Artist Sells Her Trophy during Korean Music Awards." *Korea Exposé*, March 1 2017. https://www.koreaexpose.com/artist-lee-lang-sells-awards-trophy.

Roy, Ananya, and Aihwa Ong, eds. *Worlding Cities: Asian Experiments and the Art of Being Global.* Oxford: Wiley-Blackwell, 2011.

Saito, Kunio. "Korea's Economic Adjustments under the IMF-Supported Program." January 21, 1998. https://www.imf.org/external/np/speeches/1998/012198a.pdf.

Sato, Yoshiyuki. *Shin jiyushuhi to kenryoku* [Neoliberalism and power]. Translated by Kim Sangwun. Seoul: Humanitas, 2014.

Sennett, Richard. "The New Capitalism." *Social Research* 64, no. 2 (1997): 161–80.

Seoul Metropolitan Government. *Shijŏngunyŏn 4kaenyŏn kyehoek: 2006–2010 (makko maeryŏginnŭn segyedoshi Seoul)* [Municipal administrative 4-year planning: 2006–2010 (clear and charming world city Seoul)]. Seoul: Seoul Metropolitan Government, 2009. http://www.riss.kr/search/detail/DetailView.do?p_mat_type=d73459 61987b5obf&control_no=bb4c6e02944f2f89ffeobdc3ef48d419#redirect.

Seoul Metropolitan Government. *2020 Seoul City Basic Urban Plan.* Seoul: Seoul Metropolitan Government, 2006. http://urban.seoul.go.kr/4DUPIS/download/sub3_1_old/ 1_seoul_basic.pdf.

Seoul Social Economy Portal. "Sogae: Sahoejŏkkyŏngje" [Introduction: Social economy]. http://sehub.net/policy (accessed October 14, 2017).

"Seoul-ui bam-eul jeulgjija: Hongdae ildae, gyeonglidan gil" [Let's enjoy a Seoul night: Hongdae area]. *VisitSeoul.net*, December 26, 2015. http://korean.visitseoul.net/ tours/서울의-밤을-즐기자-홍대-일대-경리단-길_/56.

Sewell, Jr., William H. "A Theory of Structure: Duality, Agency, and Transformation." *American Journal of Sociology* 98, no.1 (1992): 1–29.

Shin, Hyunjoon. "Han'gung p'abŭi 'kŏnch'uk'ak'ŭl wihayŏr Idonghanŭn sŏurŭi ŭmakchŏng changsodŭl, 1976–1992" [A contribution to the construction of Korean pop: Popular music and places in mobile Seoul, 1976–1992]. *SAI* 14 (2013): 599–634.

Shin, Hyunjoon. *Kayo, k'eip'ap kŭrigo kŭnŏmŏ: Han'guk taejungŭmakŭl ingnŭn munhwajŏk p'ŭrijŭm* [Popular song, K-pop and beyond: Cultural prism for reading Korean popular music]. Seoul: Tolbegae, 2013.

Shin, Hyunjoon. "Rokŭmakkwa 'ŏlt'ŭ undong'" [Rock music and the "alt-movement"]. *Munhwagwahak* [Cultural Science], no. 9 (1996): 175–80.

Shin, Hyunjoon, and Pil Ho Kim. "Birth, Death, and Resurrection of Group Sound Rock." In *Korean Popular Culture Reader*, edited by Kyung Hyun Kim and Youngmin Choe, 275–95. Durham, NC: Duke University Press, 2014.

Shore, Cris, and Susan Wright. "Audit Culture and Anthropology: Neo-liberalism in British Higher Education." *Journal of the Royal Anthropological Institute* 5, no. 4 (1999): 557–75.

Shore, Cris, Susan Wright, and Davide Però, eds. *Policy Worlds: Anthropology and the Analysis of Contemporary Power*. Oxford: Berghahn Books, 2011.

Sim, Kwanghyŏn. "Munminjŏngbuŭi kaehyŏkkwa 90 nyŏndae munhwajŏngch'aegŭi kibon kwaje" [Korean civilian government's reform and the basic task of the cultural policy in the 1990s]. *Munhwajŏngch'aengnonch'ong* [Journal of Cultural Policy] 5 (1993): 18–30.

Sŏ, Sunpok. "Munhwayesulchinhŭngbŏbŭi naeyongbunsŏkkwa hwan'gyŏngbyŏnhwae ttarŭn ippŏppanghyang" [Analysis of culture and arts promotion act and legislative direction by environmental change]. *Munhwajŏngch'aengnonch'ong* [Journal of Cultural Policy] 18 (February 2007): 69–100.

Song, Jesook. *South Koreans in the Debt Crisis: The Creation of a Neoliberal Welfare Society*. Durham, NC: Duke University Press, 2009.

Song, Ŭnyŏng. "1960–70 nyŏndae han'gugŭi taejungsahoehwawa taejungmunhwaŭi chŏngch'ijŏng ŭimi" [The process of becoming mass society and the political meaning of popular culture in the 1960s–1970s Korea]. *Sanghŏhakpo* [Journal of Korean Modern Literature] 32 (June 2011): 187–226.

Space Culture Centre. *Space Culture*. Seoul: Space Culture Centre, 2002.

Ssamzie Space. *Ssamzie Space Journal 1*. Vol. 9, *Ssamzie Art Book*. Seoul: Ssamzie Space, 2000.

Sung, Gi-Wan. *Hongdaeap saebyŏk se shi: Sŏnggiwanŭi indimunhwa rimiksŭ* [Three a.m. in Hongdae area: Sung Gi-Wan's indie culture remix]. Seoul: Samunnanjŏk, 2009.

Throsby, David. *The Economics of Cultural Policy*. Cambridge: Cambridge University Press, 2010.

21 Segi-chŏnmangtong'in [A coterie for looking at the twenty-first century]. *Hongdaeap kŭmyoil* [Friday night in Hongdae area]. Seoul: Manu, 2007.

U, Hanul. "Hongdaeap, sunsuyesul chigo sangŏpchŏng taensŭk'ŭllŏm ttŭgo" [Hongdae area, falling-down arts and coming-up commercial dance clubs]. *Segye Daily* (Seoul), February 19, 2004. http://www.segye.com/newsView/20040218001104.

United Nations. *Creative Economy Report, 2013 Special Edition: Widening Local Development Pathways*. New York: United Nations Development Program and United Nations Educational, Scientific, and Cultural Organization, 2013. http://www.unesco.org/culture/pdf/creative-economy-report-2013.pdf.

Urry, John. *Consuming Places*. London: Routledge, 1995.

Vestheim, Geir. "Instrumental Cultural Policy in Scandinavian Countries: A Critical Historical Perspective." *European Journal of Cultural Policy* 1, no. 1 (1994): 57–71.

Weber, Max. *The Protestant Ethic and the Spirit of Capitalism*. Translated by Stephen Kalberg. London: Routledge, 2010.

White, Merry M. *Coffee Life in Japan*. Berkeley: University of California Press, 2012.

Williams, Raymond. *Keywords: A Vocabulary of Culture and Society*. London: Fontana, 1976.

Yang, Chinsŏk. *Hongdaeap'esŏ changsahamnida: Nadaun kagero sŏnggonghan kolmoksajang 9 inŭi pigyŏl* [Doing business in Hongadae area: The secret of nine shop owners who achieved shops with personality]. Seoul: Sosobooks, 2015.

Yang, Jinsŏg. "Changsaga yesurida" [Business is art]. *Street H*, August 2014. http://street -h.com/magazine/45409.

Yang, Soyŏng. *Hongdaeap twitkolmok: Ŏnŭ t'ŭraendŭset'ŏŭi hongdaeap k'ap'e kaidŭ* [Backstreets of Hongdae area: Café guide to Hongdae area]. Seoul: Kŭrigoch'aek, 2009.

Yeoh, Brenda S. A. "'The Global Cultural City? Spatial Imagineering and Politics in the (Multi)Cultural Marketplaces of South-East Asia." *Urban Studies* 42, no. 5–6 (2005): 945–58.

Yi, Cihyen. "3 Sam Partners: Kongkanul nemesen khaphey" [3 Sam Partners: Beyond just a Café]. *Street H*, January 2014. http://street-h.com/magazine/45597.

Yi, Dongjun, ed. *Hongdaeap'ŭro wa* [Come to the Hongdae area, Seoul]. Seoul: Paibuksŭ, 2006.

Yi, Dongjun. "Kyelkwukun kangnamsuthail?" [Finally Gangnam style?]. *Street H*, August 2012. http://street-h.com/magazine/45255.

Yi, Hyŏnju. "Sobogi." In *Hongdaeap'ŭro wa* [Come to the Hongdae area, Seoul], edited by Dongjun Yi, 114–23. Seoul: Paibuksŭ, 2005.

Yi, Jeha. "Sallong padabi" [Salon Badabie]. *Street H*, February 2012. http://street-h.com/ magazine/45170.

Yi, Juhyŏn. "Hongdaeap, it'aewŏn ttaragana" [Is Hongdae following Itaewon?]. *Hankoyreh 21* (Seoul), November 7, 2002. http://h21.hani.co.kr/arti/cover/cover_general/ 6528.html.

Yi, Juhyŏn. "Hongdaeap 20 nyŏn, kŭ munhwajŏk shirhŏmdŭ" [20 years of Hongdae, its cultural experiments]. *Hankoyreh 21* (Seoul), November 7, 2002. http://h21.hani.co .kr/arti/special/special_general/6522.html.

Yi, Kiung, "Chent'ŭrip'ik'eisyŏn hyogwa: Hongdaejiyŏk munhwayuminŭi hŭrŭmgwa taeanjŏk changsoŭi hyŏngsŏng" [Gentrification effects: The flow of cultural refugees and making alternative places in the vicinities of Hongdae]. *Tosiyŏn'gu* [City Studies], no. 14 (2015): 43–85.

Yi, Pyŏngmin. "Ch'amyŏjŏngbu munhwaanŏpchŏngch'aegŭi p'yŏnggawa hyanghu chŏngch'aekpanghyang" [An evaluation of cultural industry policies in Korean participatory government and future policy perspectives]. *Inmunk'ont'ench'ŭ* [Humanities Content] 9 (June 2007): 205–35.

Yi, Sanghun. "T'oep'yee tchotkyŏnan indimunhwat . . . hongdaeam 'sunsu' rŭl ilt'a" [Indie culture expelled by decadence . . . Hongdae lost "Innocence"]. *Kyunghyang Shinmun* [Kyunghyang Daily News] (Seoul), October 30, 2006. http://news.khan.co.kr/ kh_news/khan_art_view.html?code=940100&artid=200610301829401.

Yi, Sangpong. "Modŏn p̓ok̓ŭ amagi 80 nyŏndae han̓guktaejungŭmage mich̓in yŏnghyange kwanhan yŏn̓gu" [A study about the influence of '80s Korean folk music on popular music]. Master's thesis, Dankook University, 2010.

Yi, Sŭnghyŏng. "Chayu, kaesŏng, chabonŭi 'kongjon̓' shirhŏm" [Experimenting with the "coexistence'" of freedom, idiosyncrasy, and capital]. Munhwa Daily (Seoul), August 26, 2003. http://www.munhwa.com/news/view.html?no=2003082601011930030002.

Yi, Yŏngmi. "Chŏngnyŏnmunhwanŭn wae hap̓il 1970 nyŏndae yŏssŭlkka?" [Why did youth culture emerge in the 1970s?], Inmulgwasasang [Person and Idea] 214 (February 2016): 168–81.

Yi, Yŏngmi. "Han̓gung taejunggayosaŭi tongnyŏkkwa sedae kan yangshik, ch̓wihyang kaltŭng" [Dynamics of Korean pop history and differences of style and taste among the generations]. Taejungŭmak [Korean Journal of Popular Music] 11 (May 2013): 33–69.

Yim, Dongŭn. Sŏuresŏ yumok̓agi [Being a nomad in Seoul]. Seoul: Munhwagwahaksa, 1999.

Yim, Dongŭn, and Chongbae Kim. Met̓ŭrop̓ollisŭ sŏurŭi t̓ansaeng: Sŏurŭi salmŭl mandŭrŏnaen kwŏllyŏk, chabon, chedo kŭrigo yongmangdŭl [Birth of metropolis Seoul: Power, capital, system that created life in Seoul]. Seoul: Banbi, 2015.

Yim, Hakswun. "Munhwa sanŏp yŏngyŏkkwa yesuryŏngyŏge taehan chŏngch̓aek mokp̓yodŭl yangnipkanŭngsŏng yŏn̓gu" [A study on the compatibility of policy goals between a cultural policy domain and an art domain]. Munhwajŏngch̓aengnonch̓ong [Journal of Cultural Policy] 13 (December 2001): 279–300.

Yim, Kyŏnghwa. "Hongdaeap p̓aesyŏnsyop" [Fashion shop of Hongdae area]. Street H, October 2014. http://street-h.com/magazine/81420.

Yim, Kyŏnghwa. "Hongdaeap̓ŭn pudongsanŏpso chŏnjaengt̓ŏ?" [Is Hongdae area the battlefield of real estate?]. Street H, May 2014. http://street-h.com/magazine/81370.

Yim, Kyŏnghwa. "Masŭi kyŏngyŏnjang hongdaeap" [The competition venue of taste, Hongdae area]. Street H, November 2014. http://street-h.com/magazine/82530.

Yim, Kyŏnghwa. "Pom. Hongdaeap. Kolmokk̓ap̓e!" [Spring. Hongdae area. Café alley!]. Street H, February 2015. http://street-h.com/magazine/88882.

Yim, Ŭnsŏn. "Mokkong, tto tarŭn kamsusŏngŭi ch̓urhyŏn" [Woodworking, the emergence of another sensitivity]. Street H, May 2016. http://street-h.com/magazine/93694.

Yu, Hyesŏng. "Hongdaeap·shinch̓on 'munhwa' ŭi wigi: P̓at̓imunhwae hwidullin a, uriŭi 'hongdaeap̓!'" [Crisis of "culture" of Hongdae and Shinchon: Our "Hongdae" bossed around by party culture!]. Weekly Hankook, June 23, 2004. http://weekly.hankooki.com/lpage/cover/200406/wk2004062311420237040.htm.

Yu, Kihong. Hongdaeam indiŭmang saengt̓aegyeŭi wigiwa taean [The crisis of the ecology of Hongdae indie music and its solution]. Seoul: National Assembly Research Service, 2015.

Yun, Sang-u. "IMF wigi ihu shinjayujuŭiŭi naebuhwa kwajŏng" [The internalization process of neoliberalism after the IMF crisis]. Asea yŏn̓gu [Journal of Asiatic Studies] 56, no. 3 (2013): 364–95.

Zukin, Sharon. Loft Living: Culture and Capital in Urban Change. New Brunswick, NJ: Rutgers University Press, 1989.

Index